SUSELLE'S STORY

Travels with a Trachy

Think of me sometimes with a smile.

British Library Cataloguing in Publication Data.
A catalogue record for this book is available from the British Library

ISBN 978 0 86071 757 7

A Commissioned Publication Printed by

MOORLEYS
Print, Design & Publishing
info@moorleys.co.uk · www.moorleys.co.uk

CONTENTS

i

Acknowledgements

The editorial group is indebted to all of the contributors for their "Suselle stories". Our grateful thanks go to Jane Campbell, Richard Cornfield, Dave Richards, Graham Nimmo, Vickie Boffey, Morag Boffey, Florence Garabedian, Tara Holst, Lauren Forbes, Kay Jenkinson and Gill Hall. Without hesitation, each willingly accepted the invitation, making time in their very busy schedules to gather thoughts and memories, or research and write up material from Suselle's archives, and then put pen to paper, and computer to email. The great continuity in their experience is a testament to Suselle, and her impact on all our lives. Our thanks also to Ashley Everitt, Information Officer, Disabled Motoring UK, who retrieved copies of Suselle's articles and photographs from the organisation's archives.

And finally to Moorleys Print and Publishing, who provided us with exceptional editorial assistance throughout our self-publishing adventure and helped us over the finishing line. Any oversights are entirely our responsibility.

Pat Duncan
Mandy Frew
Grace Gunnell
Wilma Lawrie

March 2018

Foreword

Have wheels, will travel! That will be my enduring memory of Suselle. Suselle and I met when she was still working as a social worker, helping other disabled people take control of their lives and live independently. I think we bumped into each other at a conference on independent living and I clearly remember her coming over and saying "So who are you then? We are obviously one of the same"! It took me no more than a millisecond to realise she meant we both had spinal muscular atrophy (SMA). There were few of us in the world at that time, as the medical advances that kept us alive were in their infancy. So, you can imagine, when we meet another person just like us, we are struck with curiosity and questions!

It is not a coincidence that people with SMA are incredibly alike mentally. Alert, curious and very much alive! On meeting we generally bond quickly. I knew I had found a lifelong friend from the moment I met Suselle. She was funny, cheeky, interesting and sharp beyond measure. Just my kind of woman!

This book captures Suselle's spirit and love of life and will be a tonic for all who read it. As a disabled woman, I have used politics to fight tooth and nail for equality and the right to be included in everything that the world offers. Suselle did the same through communities and simply being Suselle! You will know exactly what I mean as you turn the pages. Each chapter takes you on a journey and that's exactly how she would want us to remember her – the woman who travelled great distances, breaking-down or circumventing enormous barriers along the way. Someone who could reveal the art of the possible; a spiritual woman, who took her friends and family on their own personal journeys, making us all stronger from listening to and watching her wisdom.

The quote I will take away from this book is from Suselle herself of course! It was her instructions about how she wanted to be described at her funeral. She stayed true to our slogan. "Nothing about us, without us!" even beyond the grave... *"Please don't allow any "pedestal thoughts" to override when thinking of me - words like "brave" or "courageous" are banned! I've always said that I'm a fairly ordinary individual, only extraordinary in the sense that all of us can be."*

I guarantee that by the time you have finished reading you will have learnt more about yourselves, as well as the limitless life of Suselle, a fabulous disabled person.

Jane Campbell
Baroness Campbell of Surbiton

Introduction

Suselle Boffey died on 14th July 2016, nine weeks before her sixtieth birthday. She had outlived her life expectancy by fifty-eight years. An item on her To Do list was to write *Travels with a Trachy: places I have been suctioned* - an account of her life living with spinal muscular atrophy and, from 2001, on full-time ventilation. Suselle's primary focus was, however, on celebrating life to the full, within and beyond the life-limiting health challenges which she faced on a daily basis. *Travels with a Trachy: places I have been suctioned* wasn't written. She didn't get round to it. Time ran out.

This is the story of her journey told by family, friends, colleagues, personal assistants, medical specialists, faith leaders, and local and national organisations and individuals whose life and services she impacted. Suselle and Leah, her mother, were hoarders and a captivating treasure trove of artifacts was available: thirty-five cards which Leah received from friends welcoming Suselle into the world, seventy school jotters and drawing-books from Primary 1 onwards, twenty university essays, receipts, newspaper cuttings, concert programmes, diaries, drawings and poems, thousands of photographs, letters, greetings cards, articles she had penned and published, and her treasured collection of books.

Suselle did not consider herself to be courageous or inspirational. She was simply living her life. Her story is one of faith in God whom she fervently believed had gifted her with a unique opportunity to travel on a life-journey where disability could be embraced, celebrated and used to tackle social injustice in its many manifestations.

Suselle's Story – Travels with a Trachy (tracheostomy) is also a tribute to people living with disability and their families, the medical profession, ministers of religion, politicians, voluntary and statutory services, faith communities, indeed everyone who believes in the sanctity of human life and fights for social justice.

Grace Gunnell

1
Good endings and good beginnings
Embracing death and life

Suselle's faith was woven into the fabric of her life. Thus the first chapter of her story focuses on matters of death and life, and begins with an extract from the letter she penned in 2008 outlining her funeral service.

Her church family at St Paul's and St George's Church (Ps & Gs), Edinburgh, provided Suselle with rich spiritual nourishment and fellowship which sustained her over many years. The Reverend Richard Cornfield, Associate Rector, provides the eulogy which he delivered at Suselle's Funeral Service and The Reverend Canon David Richards, Rector, contributes his eulogy from the Service of Thanksgiving.

Partnerships with health professionals continued throughout Suselle's life and to her last breath. Graham Nimmo, Consultant Physician in Intensive Care Medicine and Clinical Education at NHS Lothian, with his medical team based at the Western General Hospital in Edinburgh, restored life to Suselle in medical emergencies and, in her last hours, worked sensitively and graciously with Suselle and her friends to prepare them for her death. Graham pays his tribute.

Also included in the chapter is Suselle's submission to the Scottish Government on The End of Life Assistance (Scotland) Bill, and a meditation, *Time for Reflection*, which she delivered to the Scottish Parliament in 2011.

The chapter concludes with another letter – one which Suselle received in 1956, when she was two-weeks old. The letter was penned by Mrs Swanson, a family friend, and offered Suselle advice and spiritual guidance for the years that lay ahead.

Letter to Reverend Canon David Richards
Rector, St Paul's and St George's Church, Edinburgh

Dear Dave,   *12 May, 2008*

If you're reading this, well I guess I can expect no reply!

For a long time I've intended setting some thoughts down for use at a thanksgiving service following the end of my life here on earth. Hopefully this won't be for some considerable time to come, but only God knows the hour.

I think I should say very little, otherwise I probably won't stop! Perhaps the greatest thing I want to convey is my utter delight in the wonderful life God has given me - the lows as well as the highs, the struggles and the gifts of peaceful time, tears and laughter, friendships and relationships which have proved more of a struggle. Above all, I thank God for the diversity in my life, as well as the strength to really be who He's wanted me to be – for the most part at least. I hope people will forgive the times when I haven't been all I should have been.

Please don't allow any "pedestal thoughts" to override when thinking of me - words like "brave" or "courageous" are banned! I've always said that I'm a fairly ordinary individual, only extraordinary in the sense that all of us can be, by the grace of God. The "amazing" and the "inspirational" in my life I believe have been not of me but of Him.

Laughter and song should prevail in any celebration of my life. Please exhort people to sing loudly and lustily, preferably accompanied by a mix of keyboard, drums and violin (and saxophone if available!)

If you want a summary of my life it would include the following:

- *A passion for justice and equality*
- *A commitment to openness of communication and relationship-building*
- *Kindness with a light touch*

Think of me sometimes with a smile.

Suselle

Richard Cornfield : From time to time I would pop in and see Suselle at Viewforth, Suselle's flat in Bruntsfield, on the way back home from the Ps & Gs office. Our meetings always seemed to be at 4.00 p.m. Sometimes we'd just catch up. Other times we'd want to talk about church things such as Connect Groups or Soul Food. Sometimes she just wanted to pray. Always I'd look around her front room and be amazed at the pictures, the photos of friends past and present, the inspirational messages, the thank you cards; and in pride of place I'd see the Carpe Diem 'Seize the Day' plaque and be reminded that if anyone lived that out it was Suselle and next to it would be the Micah 6:8 verse, 'And what does the LORD require of you? To act justly and to love mercy and to walk humbly with your God;' and be reminded of the way in which Suselle had chosen to live her life.

It was easy to connect to Suselle. Her room showed the love and respect Suselle had in many, many people's lives and that is what Suselle showed to everyone who met her. The last time we met up, on 18th May, was just to pray. She'd sent me one of her emails. In it she explained she wasn't feeling well and one of her friends had urged her to follow the Biblical principle and get one of the leaders of the church in to pray. And so we prayed. She was worried. Things weren't quite right. And she wanted to be well enough to go on her next big trip with Mandy to Norway. And so we prayed. I knew it was a big prayer that we were praying and I knew things were more significant than just a holiday but I knew too that this was the place where Suselle was. She could see as far as her trip to Norway and so then her prayers would go just that far.

As always it was an important moment and as always I left Suselle's place more uplifted and encouraged than when I went into it. As I ministered to her she ministered to me and reminded me of the important things once again. In the Bible passage we had just read, St Paul spoke about the greater, wider, higher God, the God who can do immeasurably more and, as always, I left Suselle with that an immensely positive picture of God, a God who was greater and a God who was imminent and a God who truly loved and valued me. Suselle's gift was she took you out of yourself and pointed you to something greater.

Suselle Boffey was born on 16th September 1956. The name on her birth certificate was Susan Elizabeth Boffey but her mother, Leah, soon started calling her Suselle and that just stuck. As a child Suselle had a lot of spinal surgery, in fact when her condition was first diagnosed she was given no longer than the age of two to live. When her mum was told this she just said to the consultant, 'do you believe in the power of prayer?' Need I say any more…

Suselle lived in Edinburgh all her life. Her father, George, was a sea merchant who would come and visit with presents every now and then, but it was her mum who brought her up. Her mum fostered and Suselle had happy memories of going to the seaside and especially their holidays at Millport. Suselle and her mother could not be separated. Her mother was a strong personality and sometimes they would clash heads but Suselle's mum always wanted the best for her and always did her best for her.

Much of Suselle's childhood was spent going in and out of hospital. It was in hospital she met her great friend Wilma when she was ten. 'Even then,' Wilma tells me, 'Suselle was a wise old owl.' Suselle was pop music mad and the pop charts were never far from Suselle's mind. On the ward Suselle was in charge of the record player – at first she would play the Dave Clark Five but as her music tastes matured Donny Osmond featured more highly. In fact it was Wilma and she who made the Edinburgh Evening News as they began a petition in the early 1970s to get the Osmonds to Edinburgh. They collected over two thousand names but it took the Osmonds until 2012 for Suselle's dream to come true as she went to see them with Wilma at the Usher Hall.

Suselle attended Westpark School in Gorgie and moved with the School to Graysmill in Craiglockhart and she became one of the school's first pupils to go to university. She went to Edinburgh to study Social Work. This was the time she was a hippy and flowers were certainly worn in her hair – I know; I've seen the pictures. Also, it was at this time that a flame was lit in Suselle's heart for justice and equality, not just for disabled people, but for everybody. However, Wilma says that Suselle's impairment made Suselle the person she was. Without her impairment she would never have got involved in the independent-living movement for disabled people. And one of Suselle's greatest achievements is that she along with others helped change the thinking of Government in seeing disability from a medical model perspective and moving them to implementing the social model which encourages independent living. Here Suselle pioneered and fought graciously and kindly to get thinking about disabled people changed and especially helping the physical and social barriers in society become more accessible. Suselle said you label jars and not people and her desire as always was for inclusive living.

If you Google Suselle Boffey's name you get a huge list of organizations Suselle helped to shape, establish, form and lead. Lothian Coalition of Disabled People, Grapevine, Lothian Centre for Independent Living (Suselle is one of the significant players in the UK in setting up the Independent Living Movement – and that is a big deal), Independent Disability Equality across Lothian or IDEAL for short, AccessAbility Lothian (an educational brokerage between disabled people and educational providers across Lothian to make further and higher education available to disabled people), UPDATE Scotland, Glasgow Centre for Independent Living, Scottish Personal Assistant Employers Network or SPAEN for short.

Also Suselle was actively involved with campaigning against assisted suicide in Scotland and across the UK. She is remembered especially here for debating the formidable Margo MacDonald. Suselle was passionate, fearless, convicted, informed, diplomatic and persuasive and she helped change the world for many disabled people in the UK and especially Scotland. A work which lives on and shines brightly and always will. Justice and mercy shone out of Suselle and these are two things she would love us all to think of when we remember her. She was a human rights champion.

For many years Suselle practiced as a Social Worker and she had a very full and professional life. Firstly, working with children. Suselle always loved children. She loved being around them and chatting to them. She was at their level. She especially loved it when a very young Katie Maclean asked her to budge out of her chair so that she could have a go! However, as Suselle's career progressed, with all her skills and knowledge of Independent Living she became an Independent Living Officer. As part of this role, she began to teach third-year social work students at Edinburgh University, and created two modules for Stephenson College courses designed for students seeking to become personal assistants (PAs) - the first module on working towards independent living, and the second on preparing to be a personal assistant. Suselle's big idea was if you could employ your own staff it meant that you had control and choice and then you could live life as independently as you wanted. Previously it was being done to you but now you were in control. A significant and fundamental mind shift.

For many years Suselle and her mum managed well together despite their sometimes fiery relationship but it was when Suselle was thirty-six, because her mum wasn't as fit as when she was younger, that Suselle first started to employ her own personal assistants; something which was to greatly enhance her life. I think too she greatly enhanced her assistants' lives. Mandy, Suselle's great friend and longest-serving personal assistant, said Suselle opened her eyes and introduced her to so many things that she wouldn't have tried without her input. Suselle employed many assistants and special mention today must be given not only to Mandy but also Michelle, Penny, Soňa, Vicky, Ro and so many others.

You learned a lot working with Suselle. Your eyes became opened to new things because of who Suselle was as a person. Suselle was a good communicator, very fair, generous and you made a good bond with her. Mandy said in her many years assisting Suselle she developed a good humour. One thing Suselle thought she was going to lose as she moved from her mother to having personal assistants was the chance to travel. Suselle and her mum had been on some great journeys especially the trip to New York via Iceland. However, her travelling and exploring was only just beginning. She met her perfect travelling partner in Mandy.

It all started when Suselle tentatively asked Mandy if she would be prepared to take her to a Joni Eareckson conference in Hungary – little did she know but in Mandy Suselle had discovered someone who was cool, calm and collected, was never phased and had the ability to drive a huge amount of miles and enjoyed an adventure as much as Suselle. And together they visited Denmark, Germany, France, Paris, Spain, Switzerland, Liechtenstein, Austria, Slovakia, Hungary, Berlin, Lithuania, Latvia, Estonia, St Petersburg, Kaliningrad, Russia (where they managed to give the Russian police the slip), Andorra, Sweden, Finland, Poland

and lastly Norway. I hope I haven't left anything out – it was hard to keep up when the list was being told to me.

When they travelled they never used Satnav but trusted in real maps and asking people. As they travelled, they felt it was God keeping them safe. They made a great team. When they were travelling, the thing they always did was find the poshest and best hotel and they'd just simply go in for a coffee to sit and watch and enjoy and observe. At first Mandy didn't understand why Suselle always wanted to do this but soon understood that always Suselle just wanted to see what it was like, she was interested, keen to be part of things, keen to understand. Mandy showed me a wonderful video of Suselle taken during the last trip to Norway. Suselle had managed for the first time in her life to get very close to a waterfall and experience it in full flow and the joy and the wonder on her face as she looked was fantastic to see.

Suselle was a lifelong learner and you just saw this be enacted out all over her face as she looked, amazed! Mandy truly appreciated all these experiences. Just working for Suselle and being her friend meant that Mandy came into contact with all kinds of interesting people from wide varieties of walks of life. She especially enjoyed working in the rich diversity which Suselle offered. She loved the culture and the history Suselle introduced her to. The way in which Suselle knew obscure facts and she held onto detail – for Mandy, Suselle was always the kind of person who should be your phone a friend on any quiz. She loved the way in which really the only time Suselle was happy to get up early was in order to queue for tickets at the book festival. She is so grateful for all the trips to the theatre. She loved the way in which Suselle wanted to connect with her own personal history and explore things like her Jewish background inherited from her grandfather. And, in the last eleven years, Suselle's background became more alive as she discovered and connected with her cousins Billy and Morag from Greenock which led to her being united with New Zealand half-sister Vickie, who's here with us today, and half-brother Richard who now lives in Perth, Australia, and who sadly couldn't join us.

Vickie says she feels very fortunate that she was able to meet Suselle and enjoy her hospitality, love for Edinburgh, passion for life, her amazing intellect, her world view, and her determination to stand up for the rights of others - she has made our lives so much richer - and the lives of all those who were her friends and for whom she advocated. Vickie says, 'I certainly feel very blessed to have had a connection to such a special lady.' And Vickie is so right, Suselle was such a special lady, she was significant, she was important, she hated being called inspirational but she was. She was someone who helped to change the world and who has made the world a much better place to be for so many people. She has changed a culture. And so much is to be celebrated about her.

Suselle loved life and lived life to the full. She was loving, caring, and thoughtful, reflective, wise, compassionate, and understanding. Suselle was influential and most especially encouraging. In fact, "encouraging" is the most common word people have said when they've remembered Suselle to me. She wanted people to do the best that they could. She was very balanced. She gave careful advice. She always had a listening ear. She led by example. Laughter was part of her life, especially at herself. Wilma says her 'closest friend had a vigor for life and grabbed at it.'

This all sounds great, but Suselle would happily tell you she was no angel. Sometimes when you weren't on the same wavelength it could be frustrating, but never for long. Because ultimately Suselle was selfless and she looked out for others. When she was in hospital for the final time and things were nearing the end, and she had just found out that she was dying, her first thought was to think of Mandy and make sure Mandy was OK.

Suselle lived and breathed out her deep, well-formed Christian faith. In fact, without her faith shaping and informing her, she would never have been the Suselle we all knew and loved. It was her faith which directed her and enabled her to live a life about justice and equality, about openness and friendship and about what she called 'kindness with a light touch.' Suselle's faith in action led Mandy to faith and I dare say many more of us have had our faiths deepened by our own encounters with Suselle.

And in a moment or two, Dave is really going to open up how Suselle's faith in Jesus was the most important thing for her. But I just wanted to say a final word about Suselle and especially her sound track which was her ventilator. At a Women on Tuesday (WOT) meeting, they were having a time of quiet contemplation and prayer, and Suselle was most concerned because she felt her ventilator might have been distracting the group members from their praying. 'Oh no,' came the group reply, 'the rhythm of your ventilator helps us to pray as it is soothing!'

And that's the thing about Suselle, the person she was, the way she tried to live her live, her faith in action, they all became encouragements to pray. Her ventilator Sunday by Sunday especially at our 7.00 p.m. service was like our heartbeat of prayer – a reminder to put God into the centre of our lives, a reminder that God really cares, a reminder that with faith you can do anything. A reminder that this deeper, wider God from Ephesians 3, this immeasurably more God, this God of love, this God who strengthens, this God who lives in our hearts – is here, is on our side, and is waiting for us to deepen our knowledge and our relationship with him.

Suselle, just by who she was, naturally pointed people to God and we are just so grateful for that and the woman she was and it causes us all to pray 'may Suselle Boffey rest in peace and rise in glory'. Amen

Dave Richards : Suselle was many things to many people - activist, campaigner, friend, fiercely independent, advisor - but at the heart of Suselle's life was her faith in God. It sustained her, comforted her, strengthened her, and challenged her throughout her life.

It was not a crutch for her or an 'easy believism' - it provoked her to think, to read, to pray and to live life more fully. It didn't shield her from the tough times or the tough questions - whether that be in a Parliamentary committee room or a hospital ward in the early hours. She knew life was precious and fragile - but her faith in Jesus Christ grounded her and rooted her. In a letter she wrote in 2008 for her funeral, she said to me, *What I want you to convey is the utter delight in the wonderful life God has given me*.

For Suselle, Psalm 139 was no proof text to be used as a political slogan about the value of every human life - although she believed that passionately too. For Suselle, they were a daily and personal reality. She knew that she was *'fearfully and wonderfully made'*…she knew that *'God had searched me and you know me.'*…..She believed passionately that God had *'created my inmost being, knit me together in my mother's womb'*….

This was no other-worldly belief that offered a vain hope in a better future - it was a gritty, down to earth faith based in God's compassion, justice and unconditional love. Three quick features of Suselle's faith stood out for me, in the twenty years I was privileged to know her as her pastor and her friend.

Firstly, her faith was thought through - Suselle did not settle for easy answers. She couldn't afford to. Life was hard and, at times, life was tough. Relationships were often not easy for her - sometimes with those closest to her and sometimes at work. In her funeral letter she referred to *'the lows as well as the highs; the struggles and the gifts of peaceful times, tears and laughter, friendships and relationships which have proved more of a struggle.'* But Suselle never ducked these hard times. She believed in a God who didn't promise an easy life but offered strength and grit to get through the hard times. She read because she wanted to know God better - to understand Him more - to wrestle with difficult and big questions. As a preacher, she was a great encourager to me but also a challenge. Often I knew she knew more than me, and she knew that I knew that she knew more than me - but she never lorded it over me. There would be the humble word after a sermon – *'thanks I needed that'* and occasionally *'I have been waiting for a while for you to preach that sermon.'* but always offered with grace and humility, never arrogance.

Secondly, her faith was honest and full of humour. When she didn't know, she said so. When she didn't understand, she said so. She knew God accepted her but also knew He could cope with her questions and frustration. She didn't take herself too seriously but took God very seriously. I knew she prayed - for me, for my family, this church and lots of people. But hers was not a pious faith - it was grounded, normal and had a deep integrity.

And finally, her faith enabled her to live life to the full. She knew she wasn't perfect and she knew she was no saint. Indeed, she banned words like *'brave'* or *'courageous'* from her thanksgiving service. She was aware of her faults and weaknesses but was determined to make the most of her life. If being alive was a struggle for her, then living was something to be savoured and enjoyed. Her physical limitations were not going to restrict how she lived her life - whether it was through travel, friends, church, music, festivals, books - she lived a fuller life than millions of so called able-bodied people. Because she really understood the value of human life - like her faith, this was no theory or philosophy - this was personal. She knew who she was - and that knowledge was based on God's acceptance, forgiveness and unconditional love. As she wrote in her letter, *'I believe I am a fairly ordinary individual, only extraordinary in the sense that all of us can be, by the grace of God.'*

So Suselle, a person with a passion for justice and equality - a person with a commitment to openness of communication and relationship building - and a person of deep kindness with a light touch. But also a person of deep faith, humility and integrity whose faith made all the difference in this life and the next…her final request? That we think of her *'sometimes, with a smile!'*

Oh we will Suselle…often. For that smile was never far away - in your eyes. And I look forward to the day when we meet again - with the restraints and restrictions of this earth gone forever - when we will see 'face to face' - when there will be no more death, or mourning or crying or pain - for the old order of things will have passed away.

Graham Nimmo : It is a privilege to write these few lines, to add to the many from those much more *qualified* to do so. And I can only speak for, and from, my own experience. That does include listening to the words and stories of Suselle's friends, and from reading the travel journals.

For some reason, although I was listening to other music as I started writing this, what I am hearing is Ola Gjeilo's Ubi Caritas, so I have switched to that. And it feels like a more fitting soundtrack to my writing.

I met Suselle as one of the team looking after her in hospital. My immediate impression came from her eyes: full of vitality; piercing; shimmering with mischievousness, and bristling with intelligence. And I discovered that this first impression wasn't too wide off the mark. In those days of uncertainty, and discomfort, we witnessed the honesty, courage and hope with which Suselle approached life. We were privileged to share moments of humour, and to help guide, and be guided, through the making of difficult decisions. And there were glimpses of grace in that room, despite the physical discomfort, and the obligatory clinicality of the surroundings.

Many of our patients and their families and friends affect us. Unfortunately, due to the nature of their illness, there are many of our patients with whom we can never have a conversation or get to know them in person. Spending that time with Suselle, and learning of what brought her to life, is an ongoing inspiration.

Rachel Naomi Remen wrote: "Facts bring us to knowledge, but stories lead to wisdom". I feel blessed to have heard part of Suselle's wonderful story.

10 July 2017

End of Life Assistance (Scotland) Bill

Why assistance to live is more important than assistance to die. Perhaps I should introduce myself to give some background context to my position statement. Yes I am a Christian and therefore have a personal belief in the sanctity of life in all its forms. However, I believe other factors fundamentally inform my position and it is these I wish to lay before you. Professionally, I have worked as a social worker for thirty years. This has given me a broad experience of many situations where individuals experience disorder and extreme difficulty in their lives, and I have been alongside them as they struggle with illness, desperation and life changing decisions. For the second half of my working life, my field of expertise was in the area of independent living and I and my colleagues were committed to achieving creative ways of enabling disabled people to live well with sufficient support. I am also a disabled person; I have lived with a progressive and life limiting impairment all my life, and increasingly have required medical intervention in order to survive. I have been privileged to receive high-quality medical care and social support, and currently give thanks daily for my powered wheelchair, my ventilator and associated equipment, and my social funding which enables me to employ my team of personal assistants. These I believe are my human rights in order to live equally with my contemporaries in this society; the fact that I cannot so much as blow my nose without assistance is irrelevant. In fact, I have been enabled to live an abundant and satisfying life to date, working full time and travelling across the world. I am only too aware that many others facing similar circumstances do not experience the same levels of provision and confidence in our medical and social care structures. We all know that we live in a society where postcode lotteries all too often dictate the manner and extent to which our human rights are met. An appreciation of this unjust geographical patchwork is fundamental to our understanding of how life can and should be lived and how death can and should be encountered. Such postcode lotteries and huge variations in attitudes to the whole area of quality of life can sometimes lead to frightening consequences. My friend and colleague Baroness Jane Campbell -- of whom many of you will know -- is an active and hard-working member of the House of Lords who has campaigned vigorously against assisted suicide and has worked tirelessly to change the terms and wording of the guidance produced by Westminster in order to protect the rights of disabled people. We share the same physical impairment; however, she has encountered horrifyingly different attitudes from medical professionals in her times of respiratory crisis. She has written and spoken of her experience at such times of having doctors approach her and state their presumption that she would not wish to be resuscitated if her condition deteriorated. Imagine her fear and utter vulnerability and imagine the anguish which this provoked in her husband and led him to produce Jane's graduation photograph and evidence of her busy and fulfilling life in order to convince these doctors

13

that their assumptions were ill founded to say the least. This is not an isolated incident. Many disabled people can relate similar stories; some have even discovered Do Not Resuscitate written on their medical records with no prior consultation with themselves or their families. Current regulations should prevent this from happening, but does it? Has our society progressed to the extent that disabled people are truly seen as equals and thus are no longer subject to outdated attitudes and assumptions? I think not, and I think that doctors and other professionals are not exempt from the stereotypical attitudes and assumptions prevalent in our society.

My fundamental opposition to the legalising of assisted dying can therefore be summarised in three reasoned arguments, as follows:

1   Doctors and other professionals cannot be permitted to allow their assimilated stereotypical views and personal assumptions to influence their decisions about treatment and quality of life. Regulations and guidance statements may go some way to minimise this risk, but if the law on suicide and assisted suicide is changed then the opportunity remains for such attitudes to persist. If however the law remains robust, professionals will rightly be challenged to seek creative solutions to assist people to live comfortably and well up to the point of death.

2   Public monies must be prioritised to enable all citizens to live equally before any attention may be given to assisting them to die. The right to independent living must therefore be enshrined in law, with adequate and consistent resourcing to allow this to be effective across the nation. This will have a dual effect of securing the safety and well-being of ill and disabled people as well as forcing local authority services to be fully and creatively responsive to their needs. Similarly, palliative care services must be equally well resourced such that no individual need fear the pain of the dying process.

3   Ultimately, if the law were to change in order to enable life to be ended prematurely, this would in many cases allow subtle pressure to enter the lives of disabled people and those facing progressive illnesses. While the vast majority of families would not think of assisting premature death for their own ends, it is dangerously possible for the ill or disabled

14

person to see themselves as a burden and gradually to seek ways of alleviating this perceived burden by means of assisted suicide.

It is for these reasons that I passionately oppose any change to the law. I have every sympathy for those facing painful and terminal illnesses, but I believe that high quality palliative care can and should be available to all in our first world country. With good models of palliative and social care, and well publicised information about such resources, no individual citizen should be exposed to fear about the end of life or indeed about the quality of life when living with life limiting conditions. Further, the laws of this country must not permit judgements to be made about quality of life when in reality this is usually a matter of poor medical and social care provision. This is not simply a matter of compassion. This is fundamentally an issue of equality and human rights. We all have a duty to communicate this to our elected representatives.

Conclusion and Recommendations

Further to my arguments above, I deeply hope that our Parliament will seriously consider implementing the following alternatives:

1　Firm guidance/instruction to Health Authorities to provide comprehensive and top quality palliative care services, with clear monitoring to ensure unquestionable consistency across Scotland.

2　Firm guidance/instruction to Local Authorities to provide comprehensive and top quality social care services and Direct Payments, with clear monitoring to ensure unquestionable consistency across Scotland.

3　The funding of high quality information services which will provide and promote information about 1 and 2 above to all citizens and inhabitants of Scotland, and which will encourage all people to maximize their rights to top quality services.

4　Rapid progress of current and future legislation enshrining rights to (fully resourced) Independent Living and to full equality for all Scottish people, disabled and non-disabled alike.

5　Promotion of equality thinking in all medical teaching and debate, with particular emphasis on the reduction of stereotypes and on the absolute priority of including the patient in all decision-making.

In conclusion, I would like to thank the Committee for this opportunity to give written evidence and to express my willingness to be called to give oral evidence, should the Committee find this helpful.

Suselle Boffey
11 May 2011

TIME FOR REFLECTION
(Scottish Parliament)
A MEDITATION

Listen.......No really listen...If it helps, shift to a more comfortable position, take a few deep breaths, perhaps close your eyes...and still your thoughts, your busyness.. What do you hear? Perhaps the ambient sounds inside and outside this chamber?

Let me tell you what I hear. I hear the rhythmic whisper of my ventilator. Perhaps you can too? In the beginning this was a disturbance to me, a reminder of my frailty. But then, people in my prayer group say that this same sound helped them to relax and reflect and pray and to gain a sense of peace. I began to change the way I listened. What had been a negative noise in my ears became transformed into something positive, deeper, helpful. What else do you hear? Is there a clamour of voices in your head? Perhaps from the personal and family situations you left this morning? Or from the debates and discussions you will have this afternoon? Or from the many and diverse concerns brought to your attention by the constituents you represent?

How do we choose to listen to these competing voices?

With inward impatience perhaps or other negative emotion? Or with a compelling desire to leap in with our own voices, our own ideas, our own agenda and priorities? So often we fail to take time to pause, to go deeper into the moment, and so to transform our jumble of busyness into truly helpful listening. I urge you to seek out pathways of transformative listening.

In the book of James in the New Testament we are advised to "be quick to listen, slow to speak and slow to become angry". Wise words indeed.

There is, of course an even deeper listening, perhaps the most important of all. Some call it tuning in to the voice within, some call it meditation, some – including myself – call it prayer, a sacred opportunity to be guided by the Divine presence who loves each one of us. I

encourage you to avail yourselves of this amazing opportunity; the people of Scotland need you to listen. May the God of peace and
the peace of God be with us.
Amen

Suselle Boffey
16 November 2011

Edinburgh,
2nd October, 1956

My Dear Susan Elspeth,

I have not yet had the privilege of making your acquaintance personally but look forward to that pleasure at an early date.

You have quite recently set out on the adventure of living, so I am sending you a token of my interest in your welfare on your journey.

I take this opportunity of giving you all my best wishes and prayers that your way may be prosperous.

You have set sail from a good port where the Heavenly Harbour-master takes a very special care of all the vessels setting out to sea. Some day your mummy will tell you about Him.

Bye and bye you will need to sail your own ship across the ocean of life, and your Daddy will show you how to read the charts.

You will have many thrills, and perhaps some storms, but if you take heed to your sheet anchor you will ride out every tempest.

When you are a big girl and able to read this for yourself, you will be beginning to know the joy of the "Secret of the Lord which is with them that fear Him".

"Yours with very much love"

Mrs J McKenzie Swanson

2

From the ends of the earth
Family scatterings and gatherings

My Family: There is only mummy and me and Sooty the cat. I have no brothers or sisters. I have lots of cousins and they live in different places, but they live too far away for me to go and see them.

Suselle, Primary 2, Westpark School

At fifty years of age Suselle discovered that she had a half-brother and a half-sister, and that they indeed lived far away. In this chapter, Vickie Boffey, Suselle's half-sister, and Morag Boffey, who is married to Suselle's cousin Billy, describe the events leading to the thrilling discovery, and the joyful memories of the time which they spent together.

Family scatterings and gatherings are a feature of Suselle's genealogy. Around 2005, Suselle began to research her ancestry and discovered that some of her Jewish descendants were buried in Newington Cemetery in Dalkeith Road, Edinburgh - not far from where she had lived for a number of years.

Suselle, accompanied by Mandy, headed to Latvia to try to uncover information about her family history. Little was discovered. What is known is that her maternal great-grandfather, David Goldston, was born around 1839, in Russia/Riga. He was a Jewish refugee who fled Latvia at a young age. It is assumed that he changed his surname on arrival in Britain, making it difficult to unravel the story. He was naturalised in 1868, in Edinburgh. David was an art dealer, printmaker and picture-frame maker and, for a number of years, treasurer and president of Edinburgh Hebrew Congregation. He died in 1911, in Edinburgh.

Suselle's maternal grandfather, Benjamin Goldston, was born in 1882, in Edinburgh. Her maternal grandmother, Molly Hannah O'Regan, was from Waterford in Ireland. In 1923, Benjamin married Molly in

Bournemouth, where Leah Goldston, Suselle's mother, was born in 1924. Benjamin was a dental surgeon and he established a dental practice in Edinburgh. He died in Edinburgh in 1949. Molly died in Perth in 1960. Leah died in 2014, aged ninety, in Edinburgh.

Suselle's paternal grandfather, Robert Hughes Boffey, was born in 1872. He was a plater and boilermaker. His son, George Samuel Boffey, Suselle's father, was born in 1920 in Greenock, Scotland. George was an engineer/surveyor. Leah Goldston and George Boffey married in 1955. They separated when Suselle was very young, and she had only a few brief memories of her father. George died in 2000, in Auckland, New Zealand.

In 1969, when Suselle was thirteen, Leah married William Durkin. Suselle makes a few oblique references in her diaries to an Uncle Bill. There are no photographs, and the marriage seems to have been short-lived.

Vickie Boffey : Rome and her ruins, the city of London with her museums, castles, cathedrals, Shakespeare, the English countryside, reuniting with family in Inverclyde and rendezvousing with friends living in Ireland were to be the focus of the trip my then thirteen-year-old son Samuel, and I were to take to the northern hemisphere in May 2006. A matter of days before our departure my cousin Billy Boffey and his wife Morag with whom we were to stay in Gourock, contacted us with surprising news - through a series of unanticipated social media contacts Suselle had contacted them. Given the circumstances this unexpected communication was a very timely and opportune one. Billy and Morag travelled to Edinburgh to meet with Suselle and make arrangements for Sam and I to meet her. We felt like we were participants in our own episode of "Long Lost Family"- very exciting with a dash of nervous apprehension and quite surreal.

As a child I had often looked through boxes of my parents' photographs. My father's images were generally of ships, exotic ports of call and gatherings of friends. There were also many photos of places and loved ones that he had left behind in Scotland, the Boffeys of Greenock - my granny, aunts, uncles and cousins. I was familiar with these people through stories, letters - George was a great letter writer - and the Christmas cards we exchanged annually. I recall once pulling out a photo of my father holding a young dark-haired girl aged about three or four. I hadn't seen this photo before and when I asked who the girl was I was told that she was a very, very, special girl who lived in Scotland. As time went on I was told that my father had been married previously and that he had a daughter from the marriage. Her name was Suselle and she was the girl in the photo. I remember being fascinated by the unusual and very pretty name Suselle, and I remember being slightly jealous of it wishing it was mine! I was told that Suselle lived in Edinburgh with her mother (a nurse like my mother) and that she lived with a degenerative muscular condition. I was also told that she had been given a relatively short life expectancy by doctors but that she continually defied their expectations. Due to a myriad of circumstances the development of a father and daughter relationship between George and Suselle beyond her early childhood years could not be sustained. In the years that followed George received enough information to know that Suselle was growing up confident and resilient. It was obvious that she was a very determined and focused young woman who had defied the odds that were set for her early in her life, that she was well supported, and academically and socially intelligent, having completed university studies and was embarking upon her chosen career working as a social worker.

The day of our meeting, in Edinburgh in 2006, is one that remains etched in my memory. Suselle was warm and welcoming towards us, and our day with her in Edinburgh was action-packed. Suselle was the ultimate tour guide, fuelled with a huge passion for, and with a vast insightful knowledge of all things Edinburgh. Sam and I along with Billy and Morag were whisked around all of Suselle's "must see" spots of the city - the Castle, the Scottish National Gallery overlooking the Princes Street Gardens where I remember Suselle being warmly and affectionately greeted by staff. On to Arthurs Seat, Holyrood House and the stunning Scottish Parliament building which Suselle toured us around, explaining its importance and its features and icons. We achieved so much in a single day. Suselle's vehicle was driven by Mandy whose driving skills as we all know are legendary and we were as a bonus able to take advantage of the premium parking spots available to Suselle at each location – the thirteen-year-old nephew was well impressed with his "new" auntie! It was an amazing day for us all ending with a fish dinner at Suselle's place.

It was at this time we were able to find out a little more about each other and ask questions of and about each other - past and present. I am not sure what Suselle's expectations of our meeting was to be, our link was our father but he had died in 2000. I answered as best I could on his behalf. I recall Suselle saying that she didn't really feel any strong sisterly connection. From my point of view we were never going to fill up a lifetime void in one day. Relationships take time and cultivation. For me the outcome of this day was that we made connection, it was a beginning, the welcoming of a new and special person into our lives – my father's eldest daughter, and she was remarkable and I was very thankful I had met her. I often recall our meeting Suselle. Billy had prepared Sam and I for the hardware that came with Suselle - her chair and tracheostomy tubes and pump, but it was her strong likeness to George my/our father that stood out for me. Suselle's countenance and dark hair reminded me so much of him, especially in his younger days when he had a fine crop of dark hair himself.

In the years since our meeting, in spite of living on opposite sides of the world, we maintained contact and our relationship grew. Modern technology enabled us to keep in touch and know what was happening in our lives – I certainly miss Suselle's Facebook likes, the Christmas letters updating life events and adventures had, and the wee cards and gifts exchanged. Suselle revealed so much about who she was to me.

I know that Suselle had an incredible capacity for leadership and passion for people. Her determination for a just and equitable society enabled her not only to create an outstanding quality of life for herself, but called her to go beyond herself and be an advocate for others making positive differences in the lives of many. I know that Suselle was an explorer, be it books, festivals, art galleries, trips within the UK and abroad, and that she took every opportunity she could to plan and execute an adventure. If it was Suselle's will there would be a way.

I know that life for Suselle was a constant challenge, and that she was determined to meet those challenges head on. I know that Suselle was a woman of faith. God was important. Life was a gift from God to be lived. Suselle's church nourished her, challenged her and comforted her during times of doubt and struggle and in her final days. I know that Suselle had an amazing team of people who wanted the best for her and gave her incredible day to day support over her years - especially her mother, teachers, carers and friends. Suselle was loved. I know that I was very fortunate to be able to attend Suselle's funeral and to be welcomed back to Edinburgh by her friends as her sister.

When a notable figure dies New Zealanders often turn to an old Maori saying or Whakatauki -

"Kua hinga te Totara I te wao nui a tane" - "A mighty Totara has fallen in the forest of Tane" referring to one of the giant native trees found in the forest.

Suselle was a dynamic person of integrity who can be likened to the mighty Totara - she stood high reaching out to others and positively impacting many lives. Suselle is sadly missed, fondly remembered and forever in my heart.

Morag Boffey : Our first meeting took place in February, 2006. Suselle was doing some Internet searches on her family history. The Boffey name appeared and was picked up by Elizabeth Hester, who is my son-in-law, Richard's niece. She contacted us to find out if we knew a Suselle Boffey and, if so, would we like to be in touch. Elizabeth passed on our email address and Suselle was in contact immediately. After many calls and emails we were invited to Viewforth to meet Suselle and Mandy. What a very warm welcome we received and had the most wonderful day, both Suselle and Billy digging into the family history which went on for hours. A very special day indeed for both of them.

Coincidentally, a few days after our contact with Suselle, Vickie phoned from New Zealand to say she was coming to the UK with her young son Sam. Our first thoughts were - How do we deal with this? - Will they be happy to meet one another? We then spoke to Suselle and Vickie, who were both amazed and surprised at this news. Fortunately, they were both very excited and anxious at the prospect of this happening.

A few weeks later we were all together at a bistro by the River Clyde. Vickie and Sam, Richard and Judith, Billy and Morag, Suselle and Mandy were all in attendance and the introductions took place. We all enjoyed a delicious meal - happy families indeed, and a wonderful evening.

Suselle had already made arrangements for the following day. We were all invited through to Edinburgh and spent the most wonderful time sightseeing with our very competent driver Mandy and Tour Guide Suselle. What a journey this has been.

Suselle has been a very special person in our lives. A great inspiration to all of us. We enjoyed all our visits to Edinburgh - afternoon teas, Christmas parties, book festival and church services and meeting up with all her beautiful friends who always gave us such a warm welcome. She has enriched our lives in so many ways, and was a joy to be with at all times. She is always in our thoughts and prayers. We remember with great fondness all the love and happiness she has given to the Boffey family. George Boffey would have been so proud to know how life had worked out for his two daughters - Suselle and Vickie having made contact and having formed a loving friendship.

Billy's memory was of meeting Suselle when she was two or three years old, that they had visited them several times with her mother and father in Greenock, and that she was a very fragile child in a small chair. Having been diagnosed with a muscular condition, they were always warned to be very careful with her. That didn't stop them fighting each other to push the chair and running up and down hills. She also visited Granny Boffey in Ratho Street around that same time and then, maybe a year or two later, in the Medical Aid Nursing Home. The first notification I had from Suselle mentioned that George, her father, visited her with presents when she was in primary school in Edinburgh, where she had moved with her mother.

3
Social justice
A basic human right

"requirements include - personal and professional experience of and involvement with a range of people, organisations, lifestyles etc; the first among equals, a supportive colleague and a thoughtful motivator; dogmatic fundamentalism is not what we need - among the skills we need to harness from this point on are thoughtful contemplation, measured consideration, weighing-up, balancing and discussing in a supportive environment. You are ideally suited."

Extract of a letter from Dougie Herd to Suselle
16 June 1992

E quality of opportunity for disabled people was at the heart of Suselle's crusade. Consequently, when Dougie Herd, the outgoing Convenor of Lothian Coalition of Disabled People (LCDP), invited her to take over the Convenor's role, she responded in the affirmative.

In this chapter, Florence Garabedian, Chief Executive Officer of Lothian Centre for Inclusive Living (LCiL) describes how her working relationship and friendship with Suselle unfolded. She traces the fascinating history of the ground-breaking Independent Living Movement, its fundamental precepts of self-empowerment and peer support, and the role which Suselle played in its pioneering work.

Personal assistance is an important key for unlocking the door to independent living. The chapter concludes with Mandy Frew's voyage of discovery during twenty-two enthralling years as one of Suselle's Personal Assistants. Mandy shares essential elements of a successful PA/employer partnership, and describes how the partnership with Suselle enriched her life.

Florence Garabedian : First, let me ask you a question. With how many people, on meeting them for the first time, have you engaged in a conversation about spirituality, your childhood and a place that in many ways shaped your understanding of faith? I can probably guess the answer with accuracy! Yet, the first time I met Suselle, who I knew of but had never spoken to, we had such a conversation. As if talking about the weather in France, we discussed Taizé, an ecumenical place in Burgundy where Brother Roger Schutz (Suselle remembered his name, I didn't), a reformed Protestant, had created a community of brothers from Catholic and Protestant backgrounds, and from about thirty countries, where people from around the world would come to for retreats and celebrations.

The topic of our first meeting was work, and the possibility of Suselle being seconded from Edinburgh social work services, where she worked, to my organisation: the Lothian Centre for Inclusive Living (still Lothian Centre for Integrated Living at the time), but we connected through sharing how Taizé was a special place for both of us. I had been there many times as a child with my family and friends who had their country house not very far away; I associated it with a genuine place of connection to God. Suselle had been there few years before our conversation, in 2005, guided by her own faith and her love of adventure. Indeed, soon after having visited Taizé, Suselle who was then the Vice Convenor of the Board of the Scottish Personal Assistant Employers Network (SPAEN) had written an article, with photos, in their newsletter entitled, 'A diary of a Journey through France and Spain'. Of Taizé and her visit there she said, 'The peace and reconciliation community on the edge of the village attracts 1,000s of people every year and we managed to scrounge a bed for the night (this actually involved Mandy, Suselle's PA, dismantling a bunk bed to give me access!) which was only possible with a willing and able PA and my brave little car'.

Like many of her friends, my memories of Suselle are linked to her deep faith, her love of travel and adventures and a great sense of wicked

28

humour. For those, however, who live connected to, or work within, the Independent Living Movement, Suselle also epitomized what it means to live independently. She demonstrated how with adequate support and control over that support she could live a fulfilling life, even if, like many disabled people, she also encountered many barriers. Whether it was about living through it or fighting for it, Suselle's life is intrinsically linked to Independent Living and the foundation of the movement of the same name in Edinburgh and Scotland.

By identifying as a disabled person, rather than a person with a disability, Suselle was affirming that she was not so much disabled by her long-term condition, impairment or 'disability' but by the barriers she met and which could indeed disadvantage her greatly. For Suselle, and many disabled people within the Independent Living Movement, the disabling process was not so much due to the physical or cognitive limitations experienced by a person but to the barriers – physical, social, attitudinal, economic – the person meets through lack of support, lack of access to many things non-disabled people take for granted, institutionalisation, and by the way disabled people are represented culturally and in the media. This understanding is also called the social model of disability. Once adopted as a tool to grasp disability, it fundamentally changes the perception one has of society in relation to disabled people. Supporting disabled people, or even caring for them (a concept many people within the Independent Living Movement are not comfortable with) is no longer about looking after, curing, fixing disabled people or even normalising their lives, it is about addressing the societal barriers that discriminate and undermine their human rights.

Edinburgh in the 1980s saw an increasing number of disabled people aware of, and influenced by, other disabled people in the US and south of the border who aspired to live more independent lives, in control of their support and with the same choice and opportunities as non-disabled people. Involved in different and sometimes overlapping networks, groups of disabled people came together to initiate 'user-led' projects, organisations, events, and new networks. In Edinburgh first, then in Glasgow, over the years the Movement spread all over Scotland.

Suselle was involved right at the start in a number of these initiatives, and as they developed. As a disabled person, and as one of the first personal assistant (PA) employers, she committed herself to the 'Movement'. In the late 1980s one of these original groups, made up of very active disabled people who were self-organisers, excellent connectors and all committed to the user-led model, was the Lothian Coalition of Disabled People (LCDP). One of its founders, Dougie Herd, wrote in Issue 28 of the 'Lothian People' that the aim of the Coalition was to:

- create a democratic organisation of disabled people in the Lothians
- involve disabled people in the planning, organisation and delivery of services
- support disabled people's assertiveness, self-confidence and empowerment
- secure by any peaceful means necessary equality of opportunities for disabled people.

Constituted in 1989, LCDP shared offices with other organisations such as the Edinburgh District Council Women's Unit Office, the Equality Council at Edinburgh District Council or an office in Shandwick Place - before the official inauguration in June 1990 of the recently refurbished offices at 13 Johnston Terrace, by Alistair Darling QC MP for Edinburgh Central. On this occasion, Bill Fisher, Coalition Convenor, made clear that through the now established Coalition the voice of disabled people: "would be heard more strongly. Providers of services, decision makers, politicians and the community at large would no longer be able to say that they didn't know where to go to hear what disabled people had to say." Something that Suselle, then Minute Secretary of the Group, and later Convener of the Coalition, defended all her life.

Suselle brought many aspects of her identity as a disabled person to the Coalition. As an activist and trainer, within IDEAL Training, a consultancy service providing Disability Equality Training (DET) to organisations seeking to fashion their services to the needs of disabled people. As a woman, developing with others the Women's Group of the Coalition. It may have seemed that the focus of the group was

30

reinforcing women's stereotypes when the facilitators invited a beautician for one of its first gatherings. It moved on, however, very quickly bringing out the collective creativity and vision of a group of strong disabled women. Keen to use photography to create different images of disabled women, 'Snap Happy' invited all women members, under the instruction of a tutor, to "take a lot of photographs of anything and everything and to attend a couple of portrait sessions". As Suselle explains, in Lothian People, the LCDP magazine, "then we were ready to think again about how we represent ourselves positively. Agreeing that we are not taking pretty pictures, or smiling faces, we began to sense that we need to be seen actively rather than passively." This initiative was one of many carried forward by many groups within the Coalition that characterises the energy, creative force and commitment of the time.

With the Coalition Suselle also shared her Christian faith and Christian activism, all rooted in her strong identity as a disabled person. For example, in the June 1992 edition of Lothian People, she reported on her trip to the European Symposium on 'the Church and Disability' in Holland and on how, in a not always accessible venue, people talked to each other "about the varied experiences of disabled people in the church life and our participation opportunities in the range of Christian ministries". Ever the intrepid traveller, she also mentioned how "After the symposium, I spent two nights in a very elegant Amsterdam hotel, touring around a fair bit – but no, we saw not a single bulb-field!"

Although not all members of LCDP were employers of personal assistants, or indeed needed social care support, the coalition had its roots within the Independent Living Movement. The movement's members were clear that a means of living more independent lives, and having maximum flexibility of support, was to have choice of who supported them and control over how this support was provided. Employing your own staff was, and still is in many ways, the best way to ensure flexibility and control over your care/support, even if it brings with it responsibilities and is not for everyone. In that regard, Suselle, needing increasingly extensive support, made an important contribution to the Coalition by openly sharing her experience, both as a PA employer and as a social worker, with its members and committee. This experience was probably why she was one of those behind the creation of the Lothian Centre for Integrated Living (LCiL), today for Inclusive Living.

At the time, LCDP, together with other disabled people's groups, such as the Lothian Independent Living Group (LILG) – that focused on different issues affecting people such as housing, education, employability – was at the origins of wider and longer lasting initiatives. These groups were 'harnessing the experience and aspirations of disabled people expressed through a democratic forum, as both a catalyst and contributor to processes of change and involvement of disabled people'. (Dougie Herd – August 1995). Amongst these initiatives some still exist, including Grapevine, the disability information service which soon joined LCiL.

Suselle was an active member of LCiL's Board when she passed away in July 2016. LCiL today, as when it was formally constituted in November 1991, is about Independent Living. Although the wording of the definition of Independent Living may have changed slightly over the years, the meaning remains the same: "all disabled people having the same freedom, choice, dignity and control as other citizens at home, at work, and in the community. It does not mean living by yourself or fending for yourself. It means rights to practical assistance and support to participate in society and live an ordinary life."

Right from the start of the organisation, disabled activists made clear that the principles underpinning LCiL's management and operation went beyond the legislation of the time. At the inaugural General Meeting the Convenor, Douglas Herd declared that 'it would empower disabled people in the process of them living independently on their own terms of reference including taking risks.' It was, and still is, about 'disabled people taking control of their own lives and the Centre helping them realise that it is possible'.

The clarity and vision developed by these pioneers of the Movement in Scotland, and their ambition, have been sustained. This is because, in addition to being resourced so far, it is based on two unique features. Firstly, the user-led model. The Board of LCiL must have a majority of disabled people on it, the organisation actively recruits a higher number of disabled members of staff, and supported people are actively involved in the development and policy of the organisation. Secondly, peer support. As explained on the LCiL website 'Peer support is a way of giving and receiving help (knowledge, emotional assistance or practical help) by understanding others' situation through shared personal experience. Peer support is built on respect, empathy, shared responsibility and mutual benefit.' When peer support is adequately resourced and facilitated, and these are principles applied, opportunities for self-understanding, self-confidence, and self-growth quietly and powerfully lead to individual and collective capacity to change, and in turn toward self- and collective determination. Added to opportunities for self-organising, however, this capacity for change can also lead individuals and groups, originally disempowered, to engage positively with others and together create solutions and changes for the better of all. One crucial condition, however, for a genuine attempt to co-create or co-produce this change is to recognise, and be transparent about, underlying power relationships and imbalances at work in the process. The Coalition's members and the disabled people of today were, and still are, very aware of this.

Still rooted in these foundations more than twenty-five years after its birth, LCiL is fully engaged with the current opportunities and challenges of health and social care. The organisation sees the original principles of self-empowerment and the space to take risks or make mistakes not only as the core of what it aims to do but as underpinning disabled people's vision of 'social care': an opportunity and a means for disabled people, people with long term conditions and older people to self-empower, access their human rights and engage as equals in the life of the communities of their choice. I know in my heart that from whatever dimension Suselle lives in, she fully supports that.

Mandy Frew : I had no idea what being a PA was all about twenty-three years ago. Then I went for a job interview after being encouraged and reassured by a friend of mine who said that to be a PA wasn't about qualifications or nursing experience, but all about who you are as a person, and that I should go for the interview and just be myself. I followed her advice and then got offered the job by Suselle to be her PA. And here we are twenty-three years later and what a journey! When I first started working for Suselle it was right at the beginning of the whole idea of independent living and direct payments. So it was an exciting time and scary in some ways too. I realise this now with hindsight as at the time I was just living in the moment and learning something totally new.

Suselle lived with her mother who had until that time done all of the assisting for Suselle. Now in her sixties, they both agreed that it was time to get some help. They already had one lady who worked part time alongside Suselle's mum to assist in Suselle's life. But she now wanted to have full time assistants. I was trained both by Suselle and her mother in how to best assist Suselle with various tasks. It was all new to me and exciting as, like most people, it never entered my mind as to how a person in a wheelchair did various tasks like washing, dressing, going to the loo, etc. It was something I never thought about because I didn't have to. Suselle was a great communicator and I quickly learnt all the basic things. I would assist Suselle in every aspect of her life, to work, meetings, appointments, theatre and other social events, as well as various household tasks. I quickly learnt that Suselle was a very independent woman who was passionate about, and involved in many things.

One of the things that she was involved in at that time was developing two modules at Stevenson College called "Working Towards Independent Living" and "Preparing to be a PA" which I took part in and found very beneficial in helping me to understand the whole concept of independent living and what it all meant. I learnt things like what the social and medical model of disability are.

Suselle was a social worker, but was also involved in many other things and wore many hats, including being convenor of Lothian Coalition of Disabled People. She was also instrumental in helping setting up Lothian Centre for Inclusive Living. Latterly she was on the board of directors and was greatly involved in this growing, developing and thriving organisation which has, and still is, a great source of support and advice to many people.

Her work was very important to her and she worked in many different fields of social work, including fostering at the beginning, and at the end of her career her job title was "Independent Living Officer" the fact that Suselle was living and breathing independent living meant that people knew that she totally understood where they were coming from and the challenges of the system that they faced. In the end it was the restraints on the system that made Suselle retire from social work. I remember her saying "I came into social work to help people and now we are not able to deliver the services or help that people need and this is not why I came into social work" so she left her career early because of this. I learnt so much through Suselle during her working career whilst assisting her to various meetings both here and in various cities in the UK including London and also in people's homes. Meeting many people with various disabilities and learning about their situations and how Suselle could help them and how she would go about that. We were also asked to talk to 3rd year social work students on a few occasions where we did a sort of double act. Suselle talking about independent living from an employer's point of view, and me from a PA's perspective, then we would have a question and answer session from the students. I enjoyed this, but also learnt a lot too.

Life with Suselle was a continual learning curve in many many ways, whether it was learning through her work, things that she was involved in or passionate about, or the arts or culture, too many to name really. Life as a PA, in this capacity, means that quite often - depending on the individual employer - you are involved in some way in every aspect of that person's life.

I also learned about boundaries and that sometimes I had to be invisible. When I first started to work with Suselle she lived with her mum. Whilst they both had agreed that it was the right path to go down to employ PAs, there were many hurdles to overcome. I had to remember and respect that it was Suselle's mum's home too. I also think that Suselle's mum found it hard, understandably, to let go the responsibility of assisting Suselle and accepting and realising that Suselle could do everything herself with the assistance of her PAs. Being invisible and not getting involved if Suselle and her mum were having a disagreement was another thing to learn, and not to express my opinion on what they were arguing about.

After having worked for Suselle for about a year, she casually asked me how would I feel about driving to Hungary. Immediately I said "yes, no problem". At that time I probably didn't even know where Hungary was on the map!! I also think that Suselle had thought that her travelling days were over when she began to employ PAs. (How wrong she was!) So, in 1994, we drove to Hungary for a Joni Eareckson seminar. I think it was a test to see how I/we would cope. Well I seemed to have passed the test as this was just the beginning of a life full of many travels over a twenty-three year period. We travelled to most places in Europe more than once. We drove around the Baltic States and to St Petersburg in 2009. All of these journeys also taught me many things.

We worked well as a team. Suselle planning the trip, where she wanted to go and what she wanted to see and the route we would take. My part was to make sure we had everything with us that we would need, which became more as the years went on and especially after Suselle was full-time ventilated in 2000. Again another event in Suselle's life that she thought would restrict her ability to travel. But with a bit of gentle persuasion and a lot of trust she could see that it was more than possible with the right person in place. Her motto in the end was "have machines will travel!" In an ideal world, Suselle would have taken two PAs because she knew that all the driving and assisting was a lot for one person, but of course funding doesn't incorporate holidays!! But we always managed. Having "a can do" attitude always helps. Sometimes we would book supposedly "wheelchair accessible" accommodation in advance and sometimes not (and at two o'clock in the morning sometimes we regretted that decision!), but, whether it was moving hotel furniture or doing temporary repairs to the car or finding accessible loos, by the grace of God we always managed somehow.

Spending so much time together inevitably meant that we became very close although still knowing the boundaries and respecting that Suselle was my boss. Inevitably in such a close relationship we would argue and have our moments as most people do, but for the most part we always seemed to be able to resolve them relatively quickly. Obviously we were doing something right to stay together for twenty-three years, otherwise Suselle would have sacked me or I would have left.

Suselle was an all-inclusive person with all of her staff. This was what worked for Suselle. She would always introduce us to new people and also to new things, new experiences, she always wanted to share these things, and of course loved it when people developed the same appreciation for whatever it was that she'd introduced them to.

Being a PA for me means that I have to adjust and fit in with that person's life, not the other way round. And I now know that with Suselle I was very fortunate that this was the case. For the most part we worked well together and, in the end, got to know each other so well that we could almost finish each other's sentences - apart from when Suselle would use words that I'd never heard of! Suselle was a great communicator and for her communication was key. I really have a new appreciation how important that is, and that not everyone possesses those skills or sees them as a priority.

Over the years my work with Suselle became not just a job but a vocation. I loved my job. I looked forward to going to work. I loved the variety of work and experiences that I was privileged to be part of.

I wish I had Suselle's brain which stored the most obscure facts that no one else knew! I valued her compassion for humanity, her appreciation for the gift of life, her interests in people and places, the importance of reflection and taking something positive from a negative situation, and so much more.

I was privileged to work for an exceptional woman.
Thank you Suselle for everything.

4

Globe-trotting

Map and compass

Suselle's passion for travel was unabated. Her last journey, a few weeks before she died, was to Norway, a country she had described, fifty years earlier, in a Primary School jotter - *Oslo, a town I should like to visit -* and for which she received, from her teacher, the coveted <u>V.G.</u>

Suselle attributed her love of travel to her mother. *"Indefatigable, with a passionate curiosity about the world"*, was how she described Leah in *'My inherited love of travel'*, an article which she wrote, in 2010, for Mobilise Magazine. Hectic, action-packed itineraries and problems with cars were experiences to which Suselle became accustomed from an early age, as Leah was determined to ensure that Suselle's horizons were broadened, and that mobility issues and financial constraints would not deter them. Leah kept a record of the noteworthy events during one such whirlwind motoring holiday in Britain in the summer of 1964 – it is breath-taking reading! It set the pattern for the future - in the years that lay ahead, Suselle, accompanied by Mandy, would see her dreams realized in thrilling escapades across Europe, undaunted by the hours researching and meticulously planning each trip, or by the challenges they encountered on each journey.

The chapter concludes with *Adventures in Eastern Europe*, an article which Suselle wrote for Mobilise Magazine in 2010, and the Disabled Motoring UK Award which Suselle received for her account of the epic trip.

My inherited love of travel

My mother was quite an unusual person. From an early age, she bucked the trend – a trait she probably inherited from her father, who chose to follow a professional career and so alienated his family of traditional Jewish business-people. Mum's own mother was absent for most of Mum's life (she was sent to a distant psychiatric hospital when Mum was seven years old.) As a result, Mum's upbringing was left to her dad and the housekeeper. Perhaps it's not surprising that she followed her own thoughts and ideas as she grew up, developing an enquiring mind and a passionate curiosity about the world. Even in the early 1950s – still a period when convention and tradition ruled, she chose to go into nursing and to hitchhike across France and Germany with her nursing friends!

For most of my life, Mum was a single parent but nonetheless was determined that I should be exposed to interesting and adventurous experiences. There was not a year, even in the late 1950's when we did not have holidays – despite the fact that resources were limited and my disability made travel more complicated than for others.

My earliest travel memory isn't really a memory I hold, but one which has been told to me – of a holiday in a nearby seaside town where Mum and friends rented a cottage. But from the age of three onwards, I have clear memories of being taken for several summer holidays to the island of Cumbrae on the River Clyde.

Trains, taxis and boats!

With no car of our own and with public transport so much less accessible that nowadays, these expeditions were some achievement. Somehow Mum used to bundle me, all our luggage, plus a pushchair (later a wheelchair) and my little tricycle into a taxi to the train station which no longer exists in the West End of Edinburgh, then onto the train to Glasgow where we had to change trains. Then we headed to the little ferry port of Wemyss Bay, took a short boat ride to the island town of Millport and then hailed a final taxi to our guesthouse. It all sounds a massive undertaking for one adult, but she managed to make it an adventure. My childhood memories are not of how difficult it must have been for her but only how much we enjoyed the sights, sounds and smells of trains and ferry boats – and the general excitement of going on holiday!

My recall of Millport centres around two very child-focused activities: the little merry-go-round in a park at the back of the town, and of course the beach mission --- lots of singing and handing out of badges. Visually, the painted crocodile rock on the beach also stays in my memory. On one occasion, we and another family hired bikes to cycle around the island, with me ensconced in the little pannier basket behind Mum.

The years passed and when I was seven we acquired a little green minivan and this revelled in a much greater freedom. For the previous year or so, I had been firmly stating that I was going to London when I was seven – and so it came to pass, although apparently there had been no grand plan to indulge my wishes! As I and my access needs grew, finding accommodation posed greater challenges, but on this occasion we stayed with a family with two wheel-chair using boys in their adapted home.

Mum's spirit of adventure

In most school holidays, Mum and I took off for a weekend or a couple of weeks, journeying the length and breadth of Scotland, England and Wales. It is a tribute to her spirit of adventure that my memories of these holidays barely touch on access issues – yes, finding cheap B&Bs was never straightforward but we always seemed to manage, even when Mum had to haul me and my chair up steps or to negotiate awkward guesthouse bathrooms.

No, what I remember most are the sights and sounds: of being lifted by a soldier into my seat at the Royal Tournament at Earls Court in London, of a sunset on the Isle of Skye, of driving through moorland with Mum entertaining me by imitating the noise of a motorbike in hot pursuit, of visiting Land's End on a stormy day and Lizard Point in warm sunshine and on the beach at Weston-Super-Mare. The list goes on. I have surely inherited my love of map-reading and indeed my insatiable love of travel – all thanks to my indefatigable mother!

Suselle Boffey
Mobilise Magazine
June 2010

Leah's whirlwind itinerary : summer, 1964

7th July : Left home at 8.50 a.m. Raining and very windy, but enjoyable even though some nice country, although a near disaster in Durham, also wiper and flasher giving trouble.

8th July : Took children to school, garage re wiper and flasher. Castleford Castle, Museum and York Minster. Windy and rain.

9th July : Left York 10.45 a.m. Major Oak. Arrived Leicester 3.30 p.m. Very gusty in morning. Brilliant sunshine later.

10th July : Trouble with fan belt and battery. 1 hr 20 minutes later than intended leaving Oadlry 11.20 a.m. Arrived Peckham 6.30 p.m. Smashed left head lamp. Mixed weather – beautiful evening.

11th July : Headlamp mended. Washed. Agoonare in Conan Fields. Walked to British Museum. Dull day turning brighter.

12th July : Mona's. Kew Gardens. Tropical-like weather. Very wet then very warm and dry. Most enjoyable day.

13th July : Tube trip E & C to Fortingaby, Westminster, Whitehall, Mall Street, James Park, Royal Tournament. Beautiful weather.

14th July : Hampton Court and London Airport. Beautiful day again but Suselle had bad moment when her thumb jammed in van door. Lovely day again.

15th July : Tower and London Bridge, British Museum, BBC Television Theatre "The Valiant Varneys", met Helen Williamson and had meal at Chinese restaurant. Weather the same.

16th July : Kensington Gardens, Peter Pan, London Healing Mission, Kilburn, Hungarian restaurant for lunch. Lovely day.

17th July : Left for Windermere. Saw Changing of Guard. Windscreen smashed by chippings. Windsor, Stoke Poges, Eton. Very hot.

18th July : Beach, cliff lift, Poole miniature railway, children's zoo. Carnford School Open Day. Beautiful weather.

19th July : Church Hammonds. Beach. Beautiful weather.

20th July: Windborne model, Windborne Minster, Sandbank, Floating-bridge, Swanage, Wareham, Confe Castle. Lovely day.

21ˢᵗ July : Christchurch, Sooty and Sweep, Huem airport. Thundery showers.

22ⁿᵈ July : Left Winborne, Stonehenge. Arrived Diy's 7.10 p.m.. Sunny and warm.

23ʳᵈ July : Misty and raining, lunch on N U L Gardens, amusements, miniature circus.

24ᵗʰ July : Left Lakes, Gretna. Dull slight showers.

25ᵗʰ July : A.A. tow as van refused to start. Dumfries, Sweetheart Abbey, Williamson, Gatehouse of Fleet. Home.

Adventures in Eastern Europe

When Mobilise member Suselle Boffey decided to drive around every country bordering the Baltic Sea, she wasn't about to let gloomy guidebook predictions about poor access stand in her way.

"Not Advisable." That's what the guidebooks said. Visiting St Petersburg was only for the most intrepid of disabled travellers, and even they would be left weary and frustrated, continually outfoxed by access hurdles. Far from putting me off the idea, I felt a growing sense of excitement. "That's for me!" I thought.

I've always enjoyed travelling - a love inherited from my mother, who as a single parent would regularly load little me (complete with wheelchair, trike and of course luggage) onto a series of taxis and trains to our Scottish island holidays. Later, when we acquired a car, the world - well, Britain - became our oyster. No longer constrained by public transport, we spent most of the school holidays exploring the furthest corners of our island nation. As the years went by Mum and I ventured progressively further, celebrating my twentieth birthday travelling the Eastern seaboard of the United States in their bicentennial year (1976) -

often trusting in Greyhound bus drivers and sometimes the other passengers to heave me on and off the coaches!

The travelling bug persisted throughout my working years, but has intensified since I was seriously ill in 2001. On Christmas Day of that year, the medics presented me with the gift of a tracheostomy (!) and since then I have been on continuous ventilation. Paradoxically, my constant companions of medical kit (ventilators, suction machines and the paraphernalia that goes with these) have increased my confidence; consequently my desire to travel. It's a case of "Have machines, will travel!"

Two other factors have been key to my continued adventuring. The first is my reliable Renault Kangoo - PJ by name. The second is Mandy, my personal assistant for sixteen years, the only person skilled enough – and mad enough! – to accompany me on wild driving trips across Europe! Together we've crossed the Alps and the Pyrenees, driven south through Spain and Italy, through much of Eastern Europe, and around some of Scandinavia.

The Grand Plan

This year I wanted to do something a bit different. Having retired last September after 30 years in social work, I am currently blessed with a bit of spare cash and some free time, so at the beginning of this year I began toying with the idea of an extended trip - a casual month's drive around all countries hugging the Baltic coastline! Thankfully Mandy was up for the Grand Plan, and so we began the preparations - booking hotels and ferries, applying for Russian visas, ensuring I had enough medical supplies etc.

Departure day dawned, and we packed PJ to the proverbial gunnels - he must have felt his dimensions stretching to their limits! And so we were off - first to Cambridge to see friends, then on to Harwich for the DFDS Seaways ferry (with excellent access and facilities) to Esbjerg in Denmark. Then came our longest drive - 600 miles to Stockholm in one day. This was a superb drive along excellent, almost empty roads and stunningly long and beautiful bridges. We took in glorious views of rich farmland in Denmark, then forests and tantalising glimpses of lakes in Sweden.

Stockholm is such a beautiful city, built on several islands linked by countless bridges across canals and other sparkling blue waterways. I'd been once before as part of a European working group, but this time was my chance to wander and explore. As in the hearts of many European cities, the oldest parts are cobbled and hilly, making for extremely slow progress, but at least this offers ample opportunities to stop and stare! (Thank goodness for my new powered chair - my old one wouldn't have coped!)

Access on board

A word about booking hotels and ferries. As I'm sure most other disabled travellers will acknowledge, no matter how many telephone calls are made to specify one's requirements, there really is no absolute assurance that everything will be as requested. The trick is to be as flexible as you dare, if possible with the strong-armed assistance of your travelling companion. When we arrived at the Viking Line Stockholm-Helsinki ferry we found that wheelchair access from the car deck was not exactly simple – tackling the ramp which led to a step, while holding lift doors open was a sight to behold. Then the booked accessible cabin turned out not to be, so we were offered the most superior cabin on the ship. This *became* accessible, once the ship's carpenter had unscrewed and moved the bed! It's not the first time we've had to take drastic measures on our travels - Mandy is well used to moving and dismantling beds and other items of hotel furniture.

Once we got settled in, the journey was quite beautiful. The ferry from Stockholm to Helsinki is one of the most scenic in the world, passing as it does through the Stockholm archipelago – dozens of small islands dotted with little houses.

Helsinki's most iconic sight is the enormous Lutheran Cathedral which dominates the harbour area. Wheelchair access was round the back via the crypt, except that a workman told us quite firmly that route was "closed". We made our way round to the little gift shop which had a spanking new platform lift ascending the four steps – the manager was delighted for me to use it, but not so delighted when it refused to take me down! Several phone calls and flurries of cathedral staff and engineers later, the agreed solution was to summon the local fire brigade! Mariit, the shop manager, expressed her extreme embarrassment by presenting me with a beautiful book about Helsinki!

Potholes and paperwork

As expected, the most exciting and complicated bits of this trip were the journeys in and out of Russia. We'd encountered Russian border bureaucracy on a previous trip when we passed through Kaliningrad (a small enclave of Russia between Poland and Lithuania). This border crossing was little different, involving triplicate forms and long queues. Russian roads are also not the easiest, and by the time we reached St Petersburg poor old PJ was limping along with a damaged exhaust. But hey ho, that's what RAC cover is for, and we spent the best part of the following day in a Renault garage, making friends with another customer who was studying English while she waited!

St Petersburg is one of any traveller's must-sees – spectacularly in-your-face buildings and bejewelled churches, interwoven by canals and surrounded by the Neva River. Although I didn't enter many buildings, due to constraints on time and/or accessibility, Mandy and I found it relatively straightforward to wander the impressive streets - good surfaces, some dropped kerbs. To maximise my time, I hired a Russian guide to come with us in PJ so that we could see as much as possible. We also ventured outside the city to Peterhof (with its world-renowned fountains in the palace grounds) and to the blue and gold wonder that is Catherine Palace – well worth the money, as was our 4-star hotel in the heart of the city. The Petro Palace Hotel was a bit of luxury with clean water and almost perfect access.

The road from St Petersburg to the border with Estonia was even more of a nightmare. Fifteen miles from the border, on a stretch of road that looked like something out of a war-zone, one particularly severe pothole totally wrecked the exhaust. We arrived in Tallinn on a wing and a prayer after several stops that saw Mandy lying flat on her back under the car attempting to keep the broken exhaust attached to the rest of the chassis.   Never were we so glad to see a destination.   PJ spent the following day in another garage, but thankfully our hotel was on the edge of the old town thus enabling us to spend a lovely sunny day wandering on foot/wheel.

A personal connection

Of the three Baltic States (Estonia, Latvia and Lithuania), it is Latvia which impresses me as struggling most economically.   Three years ago on a previous visit the economy seemed to be ascending, but this time it felt like everything has ground to a risky standstill.   My great-grandfather came from Riga in the 1850s. I've been here once before and it was good to return to the Hotel Valdemars, where I stayed in 2006. It's one of the few accessible art nouveau buildings in the city, and my friend Grace was waiting there to spend some days with us.   On both visits to Riga I've attempted to trace some of my family background, thus far unsuccessfully, but in the process have developed a fondness and connection with the city and hope perhaps to return again to research more.

Lithuania, a relatively unvisited country, holds many scenic delights - including the impressive Hill of the Crosses and the Disney-like island fortress of Trakai. Vilnius, the capital, is surprisingly wheelchair-friendly - we found dropped kerbs and ramps in abundance.

Homeward bound

By now we were on the homeward lap. Still, the remaining days held some of the most memorable moments – a gorgeous drive through the Mazurian Lakes of Poland, and a couple of days in one of my favourite cities, Berlin. Museum Island in Berlin is home to a feast of treats, including the Bode Museum which is accessed by a platform lift which actually integrates the stone steps as one ascends and descends! Trust the Germans!

Our last night in mainland Europe was spent at the seaside end of Ijmuiden, our ferry port in the Netherlands.   A final treat was an accessible boardwalk on the beach before we sailed into the sunset, journey completed.

I couldn't help but think back to those off-putting statements I'd read when I'd first begun to research our epic journey. "Not advisable"

was what the guidebooks said - "Definitely advisable", in my book!
Suselle Boffey
Mobilise Magazine
February 2010

Disabled Motoring UK Awards 2011

Winners of the Disabled Motoring UK awards were announced at a prestigious ceremony at the Goodwood Hotel, held on Friday 16th September, during the Goodwood Revival Festival. A team of judges from Disabled Motoring UK, the British Parking Association and Disabled Motoring UK's marketing and events team The Lively Crew decided the winners. A Denley Memorial Award sponsored by Unity Law and presented by Chris Fry.

Suselle Boffey amazed members last year with her trip around every country bordering the Baltic sea. Although the guidebook for St Petersburg said "not advisable" Suselle took this as a challenge and didn't let it put her off. The judges felt this was akin to Denny being told not to take his trike across the Alps. But this isn't the only adventure Suselle has been on; accompanied by her Renault Kangoo and her PA Mandy, Suselle has crossed the Alps and the Pyrenees, driven through Spain and Italy, through much of Eastern Europe and some of Scandinavia. This is in spite of having to be on continuous ventilation. As Suselle says "Have machines, will travel".

Mobilise Magazine
November 2011

48

FAMILY

Leah

Suselle

Leah and Suselle

Morag, Sam, Vickie, Billy, Suselle

George

49

CHILDHOOD

Millport - island of dreams, hospitals, travel

LIFE, WORK, FRIENDSHIPS

With Donald Dewar
First Minister

Campaigning

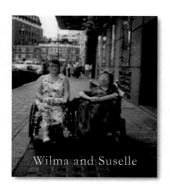

Wilma and Suselle

Tara, Samuel, Jakob,
Isaac, Suselle

ON THE ROAD

Car packed

Suselle on board

Lifts that work!

Cutting-edge technology
Berlin

Fire-brigade
please!
Helsinki

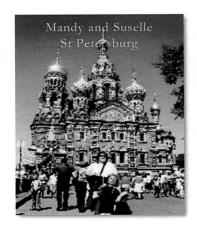
Mandy and Suselle
St Petersburg

Young singers Estonia

5
Friend indeed
A friend in need

Suselle had a remarkable ability to establish and maintain hundreds of friendships. In this chapter, Pat Duncan describes her relationship with her *friend, mentor and eye-rolling supporter*. An employer of Personal Assistants, Pat also addresses important aspects of PA/employer relationships.

Four of Suselle's friends - Tara Holst, Lauren Forbes, Kay Jenkinson and Gill Hall - describe how their respective friendships with Suselle impacted their lives and their families.

Committed to keeping her many friends, family and acquaintances up-to-date with all that was happening in her busy life, Suselle included highlights of each year in her Christmas newsletters which faithfully appeared with her Christmas card greetings. The chapter concludes with some snippets.

Pat Duncan : Friend, mentor, and eye-rolling supporter : what to write about Suselle and what to write about her impact on, and place in, my life. Suselle and I met, if memory serves me, as members of the Lothian Coalition of Disabled People. However, our paths may well have crossed in the Princess Margaret Rose Hospital, a place we both frequented many times, though – as she often reminded me – I was (slightly) older so that meeting is open to question. However, suffice to say that I became a member of LCDP through my involvement with the

Lothian Community Transport group and I remember being in silent awe of these folk who seemed to have such knowledge of disability issues. Back in the days when, for most disabled people, the medical model was the norm, a group of like-minded people had decided enough was enough and things had to change; thus was born the Lothian Coalition and my long friendship with Suselle.

Suselle was there from the start along with Bill Fisher, Dougie Herd, Juliet and many others who, over the years, came then vanished but Suselle remained and I realised that she was tireless in her urge, need, to change life and therefore choices for people whose lives had been ruled by Society's idea of disability.

When I first met Suselle, I also met the driving force behind her. Leah, Suselle's mother, was a strong woman who saw not *disability* but *ability* and I had many conversations with her about her thoughts on the disability scene and also about their travels. In fact, I turned a gentle shade of pea green when I read Suselle's round-robin Christmas letters which detailed their latest journeys. From such travels was born her in-the-future desire to gather her experiences into a book which would be of interest to her many friends but which would also be of practical use and encouragement to others through knowledge she had gained from the disasters and triumphs encountered en route.

Involvement with the Coalition lasted several years and taught me a lot. The Awareness Courses gave me great pleasure though not always for the right reasons. Cue the eye-rolling: "Pat, will you stop laughing ..." when poor Teachers/Architects/Carers staggered back into our office after an hour-long 'experience' in a wheelchair or on crutches or blindfolded, down in the Grassmarket. Eventually, this training was turfed out as being an inappropriate portrayal of disabled people but I must confess that I thought it gave a good, sharp idea of some of the issues confronted in daily life. (I seem to remember that dog dirt loomed high on the Yuck-ometer of the wheelchair-user group!) Suselle and I agreed to disagree on that issue.

On the theme of journeys – The Great London Short Break remains in my mind as A GREAT EXPERIENCE, courtesy of Suselle and Mandy. In brief: I was told we were going down to London so that Suselle could contest a parking fine and to see a show. As one does. Came the day: to all of Suselle's journeying goods and chattels were added mine. For anyone who has ever seen that trusty vehicle packed up, ready for another expedition, try to imagine my zimmer/powered chair/sticks and a couple of clean jumpers tossed into the mix. The poor vehicle was groaning. Next, Mandy had to heave me into the front seat but I started to laugh, which set Suselle and Mandy off – but The Gaffer told me to dry up or we'd never reach the end of the road, let alone London. Thus began four days of non-stop hilarity and, well, happenings.

We saw "Chitty Chitty Bang Bang", sailed gently along the Thames (though I moaned about being frozen to the marrow in the grey drizzle), viewed the river and Houses of Parliament and several back gardens from the London Eye, traipsed over the Wibbly Wobbly Bridge, visited Tate Modern, Covent Garden, the Royal Ballet, the upper levels of the Albert Hall. You name it, we did it. Homeward bound via York, we 'called in' to Harrods before we left London. "An hour will be lovely", said I. Hollow laughter from Suselle and Mandy. Five hours later … we set off for York! Next day, we were back home. Not being used to such jaunts, I slept for three days.

Our friendship meandered on over the years, never in each other's pocket but always within reach if help or a natter were needed, if spirits were low and needed a lift. Over the past few years, however, Suselle has given me invaluable support and advice after persuading me to embrace the Direct Payments (DP) scheme and become something I had neither contemplated nor wanted to be: an employer. Suselle's years of experience as an employer was invaluable. It was, however, not problem-free. In 2011, Suselle was forced to dismiss a member for staff for dereliction of duty. The ex-employee filed a claim for unfair dismissal with the Employment Tribunal Service and Suselle spent several harrowing days in court defending her action.

For several years, I had been chugging along with my life, relying on help from various Agencies. Don't get me wrong, I met many good people who have remained my friends and who helped me greatly. There were, though, many who should never have been in the job. "Carer" was not the name I would have applied to those who rushed in, scarcely uttering a word, and tried to hustle me to bed on a lovely summer evening; 7.30 p.m. did not appeal to me at all especially as I could hear children playing outside in the sun. No thanks. I became more and more depressed with this life where everything had to fit into a timetable – even spending a penny ceased to be spontaneous!

It is never easy to have to rely on anyone for even the simplest of things and, having been relatively independent, working and cooking for myself, I found it very difficult to hand over my needs to strangers. The Care in the Community scheme is a great idea. Who would not wish to be in their own home rather than in an Institution? The thought of being one of the oft-seen groups who are planked in front of a Jeremy Kyle-filled TV screen in the company of folk who, like me, did not want to be there, filled me with dread. The reality of the Care system, though, can be a nightmare so the DP option of employing my own PAs became increasingly attractive though slightly overwhelming, too.

Once again, Suselle's encouragement and knowledge came to my rescue and eventually launched me into my DP way of life. I was lucky that my PAs seemed to come to me with very little trouble, in a friend-of-a-friend manner, painlessly. What a difference they have made and how lucky I feel now that the stress of wondering who would come, when or **if** they would come, has been removed.

One of the great miseries for people who receive their assistance through an Agency is the lack of continuity of care. To have different people appearing each week is wearying; all your needs have to be trotted out over and over again to be met with varying degrees of comprehension! I have seen for myself how the lack of continuity can cause greater confusion for people who have dementia and some Agencies seem to exacerbate this through a deliberate policy which seeks to limit the one-to-one time spent with clients. The DP scheme has rid me of those worries, thank goodness.

I digress, as usual. Friendship with Suselle was a continuing pleasure. Sometimes, I got stroppy when she pontificated, "wearing her Social Worker hat" as I told her; sometimes she threw a strop at me when I took no notice of advice but, whether it was the pop-in visit, a day's outing with Sus and Mandy, a trip to the theatre or, favourite, the Filmhouse, or the June Christmas celebration – life was never dull in her company. I could ramble on, reminisce over and over, but one fact is sure: I valued

Suselle and will miss but never forget what she gave to me and so many people: loving friendship. Thank you, my eye-rolling friend.

Tara Holst : I cannot write or communicate like Suselle did, but I want to briefly share with others my huge gratitude that my three boys, Samuel, Jakob and Isaac and I were able to have a wonderful friendship with her over a period of many years.

No matter where we were living, be it Edinburgh, Hamburg, Cambridge or Larne, Suselle was always there for us, at the end of a phone-line or in person. My lasting memories of her character are of a person of immense wisdom, rare insight, fun and laughter, generosity, patience and living faith. Suselle was just so full of life. She listened and gave sound advice where it was needed. She was always interested in what we were doing, getting totally engaged with the boys when we were together – always full of stories and always seeking out, with Mandy, the quirkiest of presents to bring us or send to us. Our house is full of reminders of Suselle, from the now well-worn beakers she brought us the first time she and Mandy came over on the ferry to visit us in Northern Ireland, to Samuel's painted hand-print from Nile Grove playgroup days that he gave Suselle (he's now nineteen!) and she had framed for displaying in her Viewforth flat, to the super-cool two-man sleigh-with-flashing-lights that arrived one Christmas.

As I look out of my kitchen window this evening, on Burn's Night, I can see the P&O ferry and think of watching for Suselle and Mandy sailing into the lough on it, and me driving down excitedly once a year with the boys to meet them disembarking before spending precious time with them. I'll never forget the time Mandy rang out of the blue to tell me they were at Cairnryan about to board the ferry to Larne – nothing like surprising someone! We ate wheaten bread together at the Londonderry Arms in Carnlough, Chinese takeaway in our back garden, before watching the Eurovision Song Contest one year, and Suselle and Mandy treated us to a memorable afternoon tea on a scorching Sunday afternoon in Sleepy Hollow tea-room, near Belfast. The boys enjoyed many lifts with Suselle and Mandy in PJ (the car) with a few cuddly toys as fellow passengers also – a talking bear and a snake come to mind! After being with Suselle, we would all feel so alive and I felt 'focussed' on what really mattered in life.

Suselle, egged on by Mandy, may well be the only person using a motorised wheelchair ever to have ascended the mound, via a grassy, not-so-wide pathway, in Glenarm Castle Walled Garden, in order not to miss out on a beautiful view. Getting back down again was a brave feat for both Mandy and Suselle, very entertaining and a fine example of the very special bond between them.

We loved Suselle and we felt so very loved by her. During particularly traumatic periods in my life I received words of encouragement, comfort and hope at just the right moment from one of Suselle's emails, or something she so generously gave to me to direct me back to God and feel His peace. We miss her but I thank God for the time He gave us with her. There is no doubt about it - Suselle had a lasting impact on my life and had such a positive influence on my three boys from the moment they were born until her death. We will never forget her.

Lauren Forbes : On my bedroom door there's a bright red postcard with the words "An Angel is not just for Christmas". It was one of the many cards that covered Suselle's living-room door, and it was the one that always stood out for me when I was there. Happily I have inherited it, a constant reminder of a dear friend.

I always enjoyed going to visit Suselle. No matter how she was feeling or what was going on for her, she wanted to know about you: how **you** were, what had been happening, how you felt about it – and such good, searching questions that made you think more deeply for yourself. A truly good, truly interested-in-you listener. It was also wonderful, after that, to ask about her most recent adventures, or quieter times. The adventures – whether travel here, there and everywhere with Mandy, or a film/play/book event/concert/"other" – always fascinating, with insightful reflections and plenty of humour. After a visit to Suselle's, often incorporating some delicious food, I felt richer – listened to, understood, clearer in my own understanding, having been with someone who "got" what I was trying to say. And I was enriched by her accounts of her own life too. These serve as an enduring reminder of her generous, self-giving and monumental friendship.

I met Suselle at St Paul's and St George's Church, once we were back in the church building following its major refurbishment, in 2007. It's a large church, and at first, although aware of Suselle being around, I didn't know her personally. But when a friend, Marion Blake, and I started up a small church home group to meet weekly in early evenings, it fitted Suselle's timetable, so we were delighted to have Suselle and Mandy join us. This was when I got to know Suselle as a friend. The discussions between us all could be deep and rewarding, and we got on very well, with Mandy also contributing on the searching questions front! Sometimes we went off on a tangent, and the home group had the subtitle, "The grumpy bus-driver home group" (from our personal experiences, but with Mandy defending said group…!) I remember once we watched a video in which a dad was teaching his toddler son to swim and encouraged him to jump into the pool to be caught by his dad. The little boy was hesitant at first, but with some parental coaxing he took off and leapt into the pool and his father's arms. Suselle watched this with exhilaration and great enjoyment, living it with him. Wasn't that Suselle all over? She wasn't held back for a second by physical disability, and she lived a much fuller and richer life than many others who are more able-bodied. Suselle was able-spirited. Almost needless-to-say, her strong faith was absolutely central to her life and outlook. It makes me think "I can do all things in Christ, who strengthens me" Philippians 4:13. Her life stands as a challenge to anyone thinking, "I can't do that…"

I could go on but will keep this brief. Suselle, it was an absolute privilege to know you as a friend. Thank you for all the chats and discussions, the cups of tea, impromptu visits, the talk about books, life,

God, people, relationships, you name it. Thank you for the 25th June Christmas parties!

It was very special to be with you and Mandy in the hospital, on what was to prove your last evening here. We looked at pictures and videos of your latest travels together in Scandinavia, and you relived some of those adventures with true enjoyment. We heard some of the beautiful music you happened upon there, as if laid on especially for you. It was a happy though deeply poignant evening. You're off on your biggest and best adventure now, greatly missed here, but we'll catch up at the banquet. Keep me a seat!

Kay Jenkinson :We met first through Lothian Coalition of Disabled People. Suselle was on the committee, and served as chair, and I was a support worker from East Lothian. Over the years we became friends as well as co-workers. Eventually we both worked in Edinburgh, supporting people to manage Direct Payments for their care-packages.

As friends we met often though irregularly, even after we both retired, and I was always eager to hear about her friends and travels and she was always keenly interested in my family – remembering the names of my daughters, their husband and even our grandchildren!

Suselle led a busy fruitful life. She had many interests, a strong spirit and an even stronger faith. I miss my friend but as I remember her I smile.

Gill Hall : I counted Suselle as a close friend during her earthly life, and I value and appreciate her as she is now in her heavenly home. Suselle's disability was clearly visible yet she is one of the most able people I have ever known. Her positive, healthy self-image was self-evident. I also suffer from a disabling condition, schizophrenia, which enabled me to relate to Suselle and vice versa. I felt she had a unique appreciation of what I go through.

I always knew my hour or so spent with Suselle in her Viewforth home would be beneficial. Always punctuated with laughter over life's absurdities, we always concluded my visits with prayer, at Suselle's instigation.

I found Suselle's and Mandy's regular trips abroad truly admirable, providing amusing adventures to be recorded anecdotally later by Suselle in her annual Christmas letter. I benefited personally from the lovely presents Suselle picked up on her travels; these gifts serve as an enduring reminder of her generous, self-giving and thoughtful friendship.

I enjoyed several summer time trips out of town with Suselle and her PAs in her car. With her vocal directions to the driver, no Satnav was necessary!

I couldn't help but be inspired by Suselle's positive outlook on life, arising from her strong Christian faith. She most definitely did not like to be described as "inspiring". Yet it is true. Suselle's constant support through friendship and prayer has enabled me, down the years, to deal with and survive the many afflictions I have suffered both physically and mentally. I thank God for Suselle!

Snippets from Suselle's Christmas letters

Suselle invariably included an inspirational message in her Christmas letters – a reflection on a recent sermon, talk, world event, tragedy or personal experience.

- May the *contours of God's grace* guide and sustain us all. (2004)

- …..(world events) give me abundant cause to recognise what I believe is *God's grace and creativity in our world*, often silhouetted by some dark and difficult circumstances. (2006)

- 2006 was something of a landmark year for both Mum and me – I turned fifty in September! Not a milestone I guess I was ever expected to reach!

- The true constant, in a rollercoaster sort of way, is of course my faith life. *Everything is Gift* . Despite appearances to the contrary, in the world and in our lives, I do believe this to be true in the deepest sense. (2007)

- *Unyielding hope* – these words from Barak Obama's victory speech captured my attention on 5th November and have provoked my thinking ever since. It's a strong concept which I invite you to grapple with too, as each in our own lives reflects on the past year and moves forward into the new one. Whether we struggle or whether life seems good, *may hope be the anchor which holds us steady* and keeps us from excess of any sort. (2008)

- I have discovered that *retirement is truly a false concept!* (2009)

- Life is full of ups and downs…I'm sure it's a rollercoaster sentiment we all identify with. For me, this has been a particularly tiring year, mostly for good and necessary reasons, but as we face another New Year I have a deep longing to *pause and seek more times of peace and contemplative refreshment.* (2010)

- *In these dark times there is still hope and encouragement.* Examples of rescue in the face of apparently hopeless destruction, of people working self sacrificially together to make a difference, of beauty in the midst of ugliness – we must choose to focus on these and even decide to be part of the solution rather than contemplate the problem. For many of us, Christmas comes as a reminder of how *Light defeated darkness*, and as we focus on this miracle we are encouraged and strengthened. (2011)

- Joy is a difficult concept for many in today's world, indeed probably for all of us. Whether we watch helplessly as family or friends struggle with a myriad of human difficulties, or whether we despair as the world sinks even deeper into war, poverty and natural disaster, our finite minds cannot begin to grasp where joy plays a role. But do we need to rethink our definition of joy? For example, *joy does not equate with happiness* – the latter is transient and often fleeting, while the former is deeper and lasting. Joy is not happy clappy, but is more usually reflective and tranquil. *Joy is what keeps us going and grounded when external circumstances are dark and difficult.* (2012)

- Farewell Mandela and thank you. (2013)

- *Hopes, dreams and vision* are only just beginning to seep back into my own life after some difficult times. (2013)

- Mum's 90th birthday : This was always going to be the photo of the year! Note mum's direct look at the camera and the glint in her eye! We had waited so long for this day, especially for the clarity of her understanding. (2014)

6
Diaries and ditties
Tales from the archives

Suselle had a great love of theatre, films, concerts, art galleries and museums, and thought nothing of travelling from one end of the country to the other to get to an event. Stored in her archives were autographed programmes and photographs taken with celebrities - Cliff Richard, Arthur Blessit, Susan Hampshire, Wendy Craig, Alfie Boe to name but a few.

Another passion was books. An avid reader, she was undeterred by having to get up at 4.00 a.m. to queue for the best tickets at the annual Edinburgh Book Festival where she was a well-known face. She attended hundreds of events and added thousands of books to her library. Former prime-ministers, archbishops, internationally renowned authors of fiction, travel, investigative journalism, politics, philosophy, human rights, religion, history, poetry, food - all had the pleasure of autographing their books for her.

Suselle was an ardent diarist and her archives contained recordings from childhood to adulthood. Wilma Lawrie diligently trawled through thousands of pages to provide insight into what was happening in Suselle's internal world and the world at large.

When it comes to keeping diaries, however, good intentions and reality are frequently at opposing ends of the spectrum. Suselle demonstrates this with her "occasional" diary for 1978 which opens this chapter.

The chapter concludes with her 2004 award-winning letter on Donald Trump's unrestrained capitalism, and a few ditties which were extracted from school jotters.

65

Suselle's "occasional" diary : 1978

Thursday, 19th January 1978
Knowing my inability to keep diaries in recent years, this is to be an "occasional" diary to be written not with unbending regularity but when I am able to set aside a few moments for reflection.

Sunday, 12th February 1978 : Second entry

Monday, 19th June, 1978 : Third entry

Saturday 18th November, 1978 : Fourth entry
Some diary this is turning out to be! But although I know this isn't the season for making resolutions, I'm determined to turn over a new leaf and make entries at least once a week from now on.

Sunday 19th November, 1978 : Fifth entry

Saturday, 24th July, 1982 : Sixth and last entry
Anne and I found this (the diary) while unpacking yet another box in Viewforth. I'd completely forgotten about my "occasional" diary.

Diaries 1964 – 2007

Wilma Lawrie : Near the beginning of this book, you will all have had the privilege of reading Suselle's letter to Dave Richards, Rector of Ps & Gs. Suselle entrusted me with that letter in the middle of May 2008, telling me that under no circumstances was I to read it and that I had to personally give it to Dave when she was no longer here. I couldn't get back to Edinburgh for her last hours but knew what she had asked of me - something that only she and I knew. Knowing that Suselle had kept diaries since her early childhood and that we had been friends since 1967, I wanted to be the one to go through her own very private words and use them to give everyone reading this book, whether you knew her or not, an added flavour of Suselle, my dearest friend.

Suselle's first few diaries were, like many children before the age of computers, Brownie and Girl Guide Diaries from 1964-1968.

1964 : Suselle lived at 167 Brookfield Crescent. At that time, there wasn't the option to join any Brownie pack a parent may have wanted to send their daughter to, so Leah allowed her to join the disabled Brownies which, if memory serves me right, met on the ground floor, up several steps, in Melville Street. Mrs Ruffle was Brown Owl.

1964 started with a New Year party with games and a lovely tea party. As like many Scottish families, the first few days of the year featured a theatre visit to see the Andy Stewart Show. She also had another 'good party' before the new term started. Even then she recorded how important the church was to her and that she attended Sunday School every Sunday. During January she was 'fitted' for a new trike and there were regular appointments at the Royal Hospital for Sick Children (RHSC). Even then, something as simple as a childhood cough and cold would mean several days off Westpark School with her school teachers, Miss Neilson (P4-P7) and Miss Crichton (P1-P3) visiting her at home. Importantly, in March her mummy bought, what may have been, their first van – "a green Austin Mini Van Reg No 3051" - and she excitedly records her mummy and Auntie Babette coming to pick her from school a few days later and on the Sunday they drove to Sunday School. The van clearly gave them more freedom as she records visiting one of her schoolfriends, Fiona Gray, during the Easter holidays then, as the holiday progressed, the adventures grew with drives around central Scotland and Fife, before venturing further to the Trossachs, Biggar, Lanark and to the airport to watch the planes coming and going. Saturdays feature regular drives to the Clyde tunnel, Paisley, etc and Monday holidays always involved a drive somewhere - developing her early sense of adventure.

She also gives her first recorded theatre crit –'The Merchant of Venice' was a "good play", I wonder how many seven-year olds would make this kind of entry now. Importantly, there were visits to Patrick Thomson's (PTs) Department Store on North Bridge where she loved going in the attendant operated lifts, watching the money flying off in the tube system that ran throughout the store to the accounts department somewhere upstairs. Ice cream was also a special event at PTs. Scavenger hunts at Brownie and Guide outings to Gifford, Netherurd etc were fun.

Every year, on the first Tuesday in June, the taxi drivers of Edinburgh hold their Taxi Driver's Picnic to Aberlady for children with disabilities - she enjoyed the excitement of it along with many other children. Summers' days at Westpark 'Special' School (as it was known) featured lessons in the garden which she always noted. If they didn't go for a drive on Saturdays, visits to the zoo, cinema and/or theatre were regular features which clearly gave her the love of both which were vital parts of the rest of her life. The first film she writes about seeing was "The Incredible Journey", a book I remember we read at school a few years later - now I realise how she knew so much about it!

The summer holidays this year, with their van, meant freedom and travels - spending two weeks driving to Durham, York, Leicester, London where nothing seemed to hold them back - Whipsnade Zoo, Kew Gardens and Palace, Westminster Abbey, the Royal Tournament, Hampton Court, London Airport (to watch the planes and imagine where people were going to), Tower Bridge, the Tower of London, BBC TV theatre, London Healing Mission, Peter Pan Statue, Regents Park Zoo - the next week was spent going to Bournemouth (where the windscreen broke), Stonehenge, more airports, then heading home via Trentham Gardens, the Lakes, Gretna Green, Sweetheart Abbey and finally back to Edinburgh.

Early in August, she writes "went to PMR to stay." Known as the PMR, the Princess Margaret Rose Orthopedic Hospital was a place she knew well. As with many of us who had to spend time in hospital, our Diaries tend to record the important things to us during times of 'incarceration', namely our visitors - and Suselle was no different. She even managed to go on a Brownie outing to the zoo while an in-patient. This hospital visit was the first time she was fitted with a spinal brace which became a constant piece of discomfort, verging on torture at times, for many years as it tried to halt the ever-worsening scoliosis that resulted in several major surgeries throughout her childhood. After two weeks in the PMR she went home, and, for me being in the privileged, very personal position of reading her private diaries, I can see how Leah worked hard to ensure that a relatively 'normal' life resumed. The days after she came home, wearing the new brace, they were off to Rosslyn Chapel, a horse show, visiting 'aunties' and friends, going to the crèche while her mum was at church. Historically, on 3rd September 1964, she records going to Crook of Devon "crossed on the Ferry for the last time". The very next day the Forth Road Bridge opened and together Leah and Suselle crossed the Forth Road Bridge to go to Bridge of Allan and see the Bruce Statue and she writes "the Forth Road Bridge on TV". On 6th September the diary reads "Sunday School in morning. St Andrews. Home" - such a few words say so much about the increasing freedoms and adventures she was having and not yet eight years old. The Road Bridge became a regular place to visit along with PTs for tea and ice cream and weekend drives to the countryside. The following month saw a few car problems which meant that Leah would push her the two miles to and from school. Her early interest in politics appears as she writes briefly that they "talked about the election at school".

1965 : Early 1965 sees Suselle being fitted with a new spinal brace to try to halt the increasing scoliosis and the problems it was bringing but two days later she writes about speaking to some of the actors of the Wizard of Oz. Accosting stars of stage and screen became a regular feature of Suselle's life as we all know. The next few months to April pass quietly – "nothing special" on many days, visits to the Sick Kids and PMR, school, seeing friends, "CHIPS after Brownies", then on Friday, 2nd April "MILLPORT" for a week. Her days there were clearly happy, special ones - she writes of going round the island, cycle to park, watching the pipe band, going to the sands, visiting Largs and the obligatory visit to Nardini's Ice Cream Parlour, going on the roundabout at Millport, meeting people and Ann and Mary, going to Fintry Bay, seeing Maureen then "Home, home, home. Boo, boo, boo but got Sooty", their beloved black cat, "back from her holiday". The few months to the summer holidays seemed uneventful with trips to Crook of Devon, the airport, the Forth Road Bridge, some theatre and cinema visits and she reported seeing the Queen at the start of July. This year, the holiday started with a "VERY BUSY DAY" before seeing the giant Beech Hedge on the way to Balmoral Castle, Crathie Church, Devils Elbow, Dull Farm at Aberfeldy, Loch Tay, Killin, Loch Rannoch, Pitlochry and the Fish Ladder, Kingussie, Inverness, Culloden, Loch Ness, Lossiemouth, Dunrobin Castle, Wick, Thurso Bay, John O'Groats, Duncansby Head, Lairg, Ullapool, Inverewe Gardens, Achnasheen, Strome, Kyle of Lochalsh, the ferry to Kyleakin on Skye, Portree, Dunvegan, church on Sunday at Kyleakin was followed by "great fun at Broadford", the next days the adventure continued driving to Fort William, Oban, Spean Bridge, Glenfinnan, back to Oban, Easdale, McCaig's Folly, a tweed factory, Lochgilphead, Loch Lomond and...home after a fifteen-day escapade.

I think the next few months seemed dull in comparison but on her ninth birthday she had a birthday tea with two of her previous school teachers, Miss Crichton and Miss Neilson. Mrs Johnstone whose class she had moved up to didn't seem to be invited! As a birthday treat a few days later she was delighted to see "The Sound of Music" for a "second time! HURRAY!" The love of film develops further.

As in 1964, the dedication to writing her diary wanes at the start of November but she gives an observation in a note at the end of the 1965 diary "Gloria is a very bad girl. She got the belt ten times."

1966 : Her diary starts with her proudly proclaiming that she enrolled at the Brownies on 12[th]May 1964 and achieved her Gold Bar on 12[th]May 1966 and that she was allowed to be up at midnight to welcome 1966.

January featured weekly visits to the PMR, chips after Brownies and days where "nothing special" happened but the month ended with her being "not very well; in bed; still in bed; then being admitted to hospital" for a few days during which she had "some visitors". February was clearly spent quietly - going to school, nothing special, chips after Brownies but on Friday, 25th February after school, she saw "Mary Poppins" and the next day "THE SOUND OF MUSIC": "A THIRD TIME. GREAT, HOORAY! HURRAY!!"

Early in March, she describes getting her first transistor radio but the rest of the month is generally "nothing special". The Easter holidays saw the intrepid duo setting off after school and stopping at Moffat, Carlisle, Kendal and a Service Area before driving to Chester. (It was also the Election Day). The expedition continued to Wellington, Shropshire, Bristol, Carbis Bay where they stayed in a chalet for a few days and met up with Canadian friends. Whilst there, visits were made to Land's End, St Ives, the Lizard, Telstar, Falmouth before heading home via Bristol, Wales, and Chester stopping "at two service areas and Wigan. Got home "Boo". The next few days must have seemed like an anticlimax as they are recorded as "nothing special" other than "chips after Brownies" and the discovery of a new pet shop in Corstorphine. The late spring and early summer months featured hospital appointments, school, church, Brownies and Saturday cinema visits. It is interesting to note that browsing through the 1964, 1965 and 1966 diaries, it has taken me through thirty months before I have found her first spelling mistake "Chironomo's Revenge" rather than "Geronomo's Revenge" which she had seen along with "That Darn Cat" - not bad for a young girl who isn't yet ten years old. That is the Suselle I knew and loved, attention to detail, perfect spelling and correct grammar were important in all she did.

As she gets a little older, Goldbergs Department Store at Tollcross has become a place for regular shopping trips and to say hello to the birds in the rooftop aviary with Leah, aunties and friends. A few days before the end of the summer holidays another trip exploring Scotland but based on a farm, took place over six days taking in Perth, Dundee, Arbroath, Montrose, Stonehaven, Aberdeen, Fyvie, Turriff, Macduff, the Flower Show at Banff, Portsoy, Methlick, Fraserburgh, Peterhead, Ellon, Huntley, Aberlour, Craigellachie, Grantown-on-Spey, Aberdeen, Pitmedden Garden sadly coming home via a Milk Bar (the 60s equivalent of MacDonalds), Barrie's birthplace and Crathes Castle. Day trips to the waterfalls at Cramond, North Berwick, Edinburgh Zoo, the Botanics, Galashiels, Abbotsford and Selkirk (where she got her new school bag for the next school year).

Suselle's birthdays as an adult usually involved going on holiday to foreign countries and I see this birthday travel bug was started with Leah. At school, her birthday would be marked with a cake and "lolly" and the first Friday after her birthday meant driving to Ayr, for example, to see Burn's Cottage, funfairs, Culzean Castle, Dalmellington, Girvan, Newton

Stewart, New Galloway, various pet shops, Prestwick Airport, Troon beach, Kilmarnock and home ("boo" or as it would be marked now ☹). Suselle was delighted a week after her tenth birthday to get the toy of 1966 'Spirograph' and I remember many happy times for both of us throughout our childhood, along with the majority of other children, designing amazing pictures with 'Spirograph'. Ah, those were the days.

On 2nd October 1966 there is a mention of going to a Muscular Dystrophy Group (MDG) meeting. In 1965, a few entries on Saturdays had just said MDG so perhaps she was going to 'fun days' with other children with neuromuscular conditions while her mum benefitted from engaging and gaining advice with other parents. I hope that the group was able to give support to Leah. Throughout her life, Suselle was plagued with chest infections and the autumn/winter of 1966 was no different - her brief diary entries of "cough", off school, in bed, still in bed, up in afternoon, up before dinner, up all day, then going back to school three days later are a telling story of what was to come in future years but also demonstrate her and Leah's resilience and desire to maintain a 'normal' life and 'chips after Brownies' confirms this.

1967 : This year's Brownie diary shows that she gained her Golden Hand on 25th April 1967. Suselle, now ten, was allowed up at midnight to see in 1967 and on the fifth she went into hospital for a few days, recording in her diary that she had visitors every day. Sooty, her cat, is a regular feature over the years.

I wonder if the first half of 1967 was a bad time for Leah as Suselle's Diaries make mention of regular visits from various adults on different days of the week, but not her mother - Miss Horsburgh, Jenny, Kim, Children's Shelter, Betty, Aunty May, the Owen's, schoolteachers Miss Crichton and Miss Neilson, "grandpa in bed", Betty...and many more days only giving names. On 27th May she writes "Davidson Clinic Summer Fete".

The weeks passed with school, Brownies, visits from and to family friends, hospital appointments and "grandpa took me for a walk" being a stand out day. The Easter holidays meant going to spend time with her friends in Millport, going to Macari's and Nardini's Ice Cream parlours, returning home after a week, and having days out with her grandpa to a cemetery.

The start of the school summer holidays saw the duo off to Chester where they saw "lots of mum's old friends", Bristol, travelling around South Wales before returning to Bristol for a week, including seeing "Mrs Boffey" in Oswestry. The day after they got home they went to the Christian Fellowship Healing Halls of Rosehall Church. Later that same week, grandma and grandpa came home and she went for a walk to the shops with grandpa.

In October, she joined the Church Guides with Ann. On 6th December she went into hospital for nearly two weeks with her mum and others visiting every day, getting home in time to go to the school Christmas party in the afternoon and school concert the next day. She went to the Candlelight Service and writes about opening her presents at 12.05 a.m., and the whole family came during the day.

1968 : Her address is now 50 Balgreen Road. She saw the New Year in again and spends the first few days of the year papering her doll's house. Clearly over the past year the situation with her scoliosis had worsened and on 15th January she went into the PMR hospital for, what would turn out to be, a very prolonged stay and this is where Suselle and I first became friends when I broke my femur at the hospital physio, although we vaguely knew each other at school when I started there in August 1967. In mid January, the first of many spinal plaster casts was put on, followed the next day by x-rays, the following day brought a visit to the City Hospital for 'breathing tests', while the cast was windowed to make breathing a little easier. To give an idea of how tortuous this experience could be she also describes having the cast cut at her ear. The following day she got up "for a wee while" and then had the first major operation on the 26th. Throughout this hospital stay, Leah, visitors or nurses must have written in her diary who her visitors were. All of the teachers and some pupils from school visit at different times over the following weeks and months. She has another operation at the beginning of March, the same day that her grandpa went into hospital. By the first week of April, she was again able to write her diary herself and two days later had the plaster cast changed which meant that by the end of the week she was able to be lifted into her chair for the first time in several weeks and 'came home' on the eighteenth. Her mum never missed a day visiting her but I notice an 'Uncle Bill' being mentioned as someone who visited a few times a week with Leah and I wonder if this is Mr Durkin to whom Leah was briefly married. She had to go back into the PMR for treatment to a pressure sore - a danger with the type of cast she had to have. Her mum visited every day except on 26th May probably because she writes that her grandpa died the next day. Childhood diaries can be very revealing in their simplicity as a missing name thereafter is her mum, Leah, although Uncle Bill continues to visit every day. On the Friday, 31st May she writes 'mum went into hospital' and a different hand writes her 'visitors daily list' in her diary. Uncle Bill become UB! Her mum visits briefly on 4th June and, movingly two days later for the first time 'NO-ONE!' is recorded. After nearly seven weeks lying flat, the window in the cast is filled in and she is able to get up briefly again on 21st June. Her 'MUM!', who is still in hospital visits for the first time in almost three weeks and the diary shows that 'Mum' visited again on 29th June as she is 'out of hospital'. Through the time Leah is in hospital, it is testament to Suselle and her circle of support that there were only two or three days where nobody came to visit her. As visiting times were only 3.00 p.m.-4.00 p.m. and 7.00 p.m.-8.00 p.m. Monday to Friday and 3.00 p.m.-4.30 p.m. at weekends (if I remember correctly) this must have been very hard as my memories were of always looking at the door to Ward 2 to see what visitors we were going to get. Leah returned to her usual daily visits and on 6th and 7th July took her for a walk to Morningside and home for tea on seventh but she had to return to hospital in the evening. Saturday 13th July 1968 was a special day - underlined HOME! She went to church the next day and at the end of the week, visited the museum for the first time in many months. Clearly and understandably reading the diaries, she had become institutionalised as the empty days and weeks that followed at home were described as 'nothing special'. 29th July sees her last entry for 1968 – 'PMR check up'.

There is no diary for 1969 but in a notebook she writes the Sunday verses from Keynotes for a few services.

1970 : This year's diary - the Lett's Schoolgirl Diary, shows a growing maturity and as with ALL her diaries, correct spelling, punctuation and grammar are shown. They have moved again - to 8 Smithfield Street - but a large part of the year involves looking at houses trying to find the right one and she still goes, like me, to Westpark 'Special' School. As with every

74

child of the time, we were all obsessed with the space age and going to the Moon, her diary starts with MEN ON THE MOON Apollo XI Neil Armstrong, "Buzz" Aldrin, (Michael Collins) 21st July 1969, 19th-20th November 1969, Apollo XII Pete Conrad, Alan Bean, (Richard Gordon).

Suselle's love of cinema and theatre is clearly demonstrated and her critiques more 'honest' – 2nd January "Saw Disney's 'Swiss Family Robinson' and 'Greyfriar's Bobby' at La Scala. Seen latter before, but sincerely enjoyed both." The following day "Saw Edinburgh People's Theatre's 'The Glass Slipper' at Churchill Theatre, with MDG [muscular dystrophy group]. Tea after. Not as good as other years." As I write this, I can almost hear Suselle damning them with faint praise.

The first week of 1970 indicates the increasingly 'difficult' relationship between Leah and Suselle with the first inclination on Sunday : "Mum got involved with the Young People's Fellowship (YPF) speaker - schoolteacher", the following day 'Terrific row with Mum' of which there were many more through the years following, some of which lasted all night. That whole week saw heavy snow meaning that she couldn't get to school but Leah picked up work from the school which Suselle appeared to do. Her diary shows that the Biafra war ended on 12th January. Sniffly colds meant several days off school, during which she did homework, jigsaws and reviewed films she watched on TV. Her commitment to faith grows with homework and Scripture being part of her Sundays. School didn't seem to be giving her the stimulation she needed as she describes days as tedious, boring and so on, but a highlight was the 'super film' "2001 - A Space Odyssey". In many ways, Suselle was like any other young teenager of the time collecting stamps, ordering records from Boots, watching television programmes that became icons of the time: 'The Champions', 'The Virginian', 'The Misfit', 'Doomwatch', 'Bonanza', 'Star Trek', 'Callan', 'Ironside', 'Mission Impossible', etc including a programme "Protecting Our Rights" something she became more and more passionate about as school turned to university and work in the years to come.

The early months of the year had several telling entries about her relationship with Mr Durkin – 'Mum's anniversary. Both liked my card and picture.' They went to "Hello Dolly" in evening. "Alice, Gina and I went in afternoon. Barbra Streisand - super!" Many years later she was to see Ms Streisand in concert. Later in the month 'I got dumped - while they went to see "War and Peace"'. Clearly, money was tight at this time: getting to the Forth Road Bridge to discover they didn't have enough money for the toll, the car would break down meaning long walks home as public transport was not only expensive but also inaccessible. Easter school holidays only meant a few days away rather the two weeks previously but her mum still found enough money to replace her radio which I remember her bringing to school and playing 'secretly' in class. Suselle, ever the rebellious one, pushing boundaries and creating new ones.

Her strong 'will' comes across at school - rows with classmate, Fiona, got a lecture from Mrs Bennett (her headteacher) about hard work, which she clearly took to heart as in the following days she describes 'Work! Work!! Work!!!' followed the next day by 'stayed off school because everyone else did (off work!)'.

April saw Apollo 13 which gripped the world for several days and Suselle records: "Tuesday, 14th April   Danger on Apollo 13! Not able to land on moon because fuel is hit by meteor? Critical burn tomorrow. (The Budget - not much change). 15th April Burn went OK but another one needed tomorrow or else spacecraft would drift in space (LEM being used as lifeboat). 16th April Apollo 13 bang on course for Earth, but many dangers still to overcome. Emergency splashdown due Friday. Friday 17th April Apollo 13 splashed down. All men safe and well."

The spinal fusion of 1968 had helped Suselle, as she describes learning to type, baking, knitting, the delight and surprise of hitting the archery target in PE. The diary also gives a child's awareness that Leah was struggling as there are several entries saying that "mum was tired so stayed off school/skipped school again."

The 8th June is a Red Letter Day as she is told by the spinal consultant at the PMR that she doesn't need to go back, the celebrations involve tea in a café at Morningside and going to bed early as she had to be up early for the annual Taxi Drivers' Outing. Later that week she had her picture taken with a monkey at Wallyford Gala. The end of the summer term coincides with getting a 'new, oversized wheelchair' which brings back long forgotten memories for me too of receiving new chairs which never fitted properly as our parents were told we would grow into them...even if it took several years and meant long uncomfortable days!

The summer of 1970 seemed to involve her in tidying, organizing and packing boxes at home. As I write this in 2017 I am wondering if these are some of the boxes that Mandy and others were finally getting round to sorting after Suselle died, having 'lived a good life'.

The summer holidays were to the West for a few days with trips to Loch Lomond, Dunoon, Glasgow, Millport followed by a couple of days at the 'Paraplegic Commonwealth Games' at Meadowbank, the Commonwealth Pool, walks along the canal, to Harrison Park, shopping, church and critiquing films on TV.

The new school year sees the return "to the torture - house, school, ugh" but she notes that Ralph, Derek and Wilma moved up to join her, Fiona, Joan and Grace in the Secondary Department which consisted of one class under the leadership of Mrs Wills. August sees her growing rebelliousness when she 'drank ginger ale in Balgreen Library' AND on the same day 'put a lot of cosmetics on, before going to Aunty Helen's'. Early September she 'saw and tried new bus for wheelchairs' which eventually arrived at school in November meaning that Leah didn't have to take her to and from school every day. Her positive language use around disability issues would come several years later as she got involved in disability rights and politics. The other positives this month were that she saw their new home at 12 Dalkeith Road, for the first time, started going to the Church of Christ and their Bible Class, saw lots of Cliff Richard (mmm! she writes) and Glen Campbell on TV as well as the Celtic football team when they were in Fife one Saturday.

This year, the diary entries end mid-November.

1974 : Life and diaries are very different. Each day-to-a-page is filled with tiny writing and lots of detail about her life, TV and radio programmes watched and heard, films and their actors, the classic and pop music of the day.

She has the new-found freedom of her first power wheelchair. 2nd January. "It's still a strange sensation, trundling along by myself!" While Leah was with her, she could go her own way, which she did "Going home, I went one way round 'our' block and Mum, the other!" A few words that say so much.

In her adult life, mice became an occasional topic of her Christmas letters, but I have just found their first diary mention on 5th January when Leah woke her up to the news that she'd found a half chewed mouse in the kitchen..oh, Sooty! Her mail that day consisted of a letter from her friend Ruth, a newsletter and a letter from Universities and Colleges Admissions Services (UCAS) informing her that she would need 2 Bs and a C for the Arts Course at university.

1974 sees the last year at school and the big adventure of going to Edinburgh University. For me going through the diaries from this year on becomes harder in a few ways, most of which will be mentioned as we progress but the first issue is that Suselle liked to get her money's worth out of a diary - not quite the WWI scenario where soldiers would send postcards and letters in very small writing and using all of the paper by writing vertically and horizontally. Suselle's diary is A6 size, unlined, day to a page with around twenty-six lines full at the start increasing to over thirty-six lines as the year went on and, just to get even more in, she overwrites extra information in red ink as opposed to the usual blue! Please bear with me.

She starts the year writing that it is "still a strange sensation trundling along by myself" and, dedicated as ever to studying, she is doing Geometry revision before the new term starts. She continues to note down the programmes watched but now in even more detail with her diary being like an edition of the Radio Times in places. On 5th January 1974 she gets a letter from UCAS confirming that she needs 2 Bs and a C for the Arts Course she wants to do. The first Sunday of 1974 sees Suselle at St Leonard's Church, down the road from their new home, which didn't get a good crit - "long service, couldn't see a thing. The communion was very disorganised, the wine was alcoholic. (Mum thinks it was sherry!) Coming home, I went the long way round the block" - this was to be the ongoing story of Suselle's travels in her adult life as Mandy and many others will confirm - "(Mum went straight home) and met up with two old ladies who said I was 'clever'!" The rest of the day was spent getting ready for the new term.

Monday, 6th January 1974. The day started with double Maths which was "hard work" but her class teacher, Miss Elspeth Strang, assisted her with completing her UCCA card and Ian Elfick, headteacher, admitted 'jokingly' that he wasn't over-enthusiastic about teaching her - with hindsight, I'm not so sure he was joking at times! She also notes that 'Wilma's on a diet'…I still am to this day…still as unsuccessful.

A couple of days later she says Miss Strang had a chat with her 'about her worries' and how she thought Leah had been on the phone. Later that evening she writes that she had a bit of an upset with mum (an almost daily occurrence by this stage) and writes that she has "a horrid feeling there's divorce in the air".

A few days later she writes of "a strange tho' quite pleasant dream - the Osmonds gave a concert in our church hall - but it didn't look like the hall, and the concert wasn't mobbed by 'weenyboppers'! Super experience!" and ever hopeful, like me, of meeting them sometime.

Throughout her last couple of terms at school, she shows varying degrees of commitment and critique - the Rev Balfour came in to teach RE but, interestingly in Suselle's mind, there was only one mention of God in one lesson and in another, near to the election, she was not happy that he discussed the election instead of RE. As with any sixth-year student in the run up to final exams before the next big step into adult life, university, Suselle stresses about struggling with trigonometry, with studying but enjoying distracting Mr Elfick, her Headteacher, who taught her European and North American Geography, by getting into debates about politics and what was wrong with the world. I think Suselle won most of the debates and was clearly but, unknowingly, preparing for the rest of her life.

In the run up to the exams, she writes "Did an Ordnance Survey paper this morning and a statistical question which I took to Mr Elfick to mark - he said his way of marking was to throw the papers as far as he could - the one that got furthest got the most marks!! He gave me **9** out of a poss 20= 45%… He took us for RE as Mr Balfour had a 'previous engagement'. Great fun with Mr E however, we discussed 1) the election and 2) how we might spend £100 for the school. He mentioned a <u>boat</u> and I asked him why - for himself to muck about in!". The next day she writes that Miss Strang went over the first question of her Ordnance Survey paper and gave her 27/32! This clearly spurred her on as she then writes that "Maths was ok today…I could do it". Secretly, I think she had a wee crush on our headteacher as she writes about him quite frequently.

The day after her Higher English exam she writes of going to school with her powerchair for the first time, meaning she finally had the freedom to explore and wander around the school without depending on others to take her. Clearly, in April, Leah was finding life stressful perhaps around her divorce or an early portent of what was to come in her later life, their arguments seemed to be 'major' most of the time.

Her diaries continue to offer critiques of TV programmes watched, films seen, concerts attended and music heard.

Even then, Suselle encouraged and supported me in my developing swimming 'career' writing of going to watch me at a competition in Glenrothes (got lost…but who doesn't) and complaining, along with many others apparently, when I was disqualified in one final for "swimming too fast". I have no recollection of that.

The day after her last school exam on 9th May 1974, her diary page starts with "Don't have to do any work now if I don't want to!" But she did manage to get her Maths teacher to help her make a long skirt from fabric Leah and her chose the day before, so that she could wear it to the Andy Williams and Michel Legrand concert that evening at the Usher Hall. She got backstage after the concert - a regular occurrence- but wasn't able to get her photo with him, just an autograph without meeting him. The following day, while shopping in town with Leah, they were "hailed by the actor Vivien (Heilbron), had a pleasant chat and got her autograph!!" Vivien's parents had been friends of Leah's, with Vivien remaining a friend for many years thereafter. That evening, they managed to get last minute tickets to see another idol of the time, Nana Mouskouri, and the steward who had stopped her getting photos with Andy Williams managed to get her backstage to get them with Nana. A few days later, she again managed to get a concert ticket, this time to see Steeleye Span, not such a good seat but she managed to see them arriving. Her critique - "the first band was Gryphon, medieval rock, great, but a shade too long? During the interval our steward friend came and spoke". Concert-going was a different experience then as she writes of going backstage with everyone wandering around. She got the groups' autographs…three times over and chatted to most of them, a practice which she became adept at!

During her last few whirlwind of activity-filled weeks at school, she had her first 'big experience' of public speaking as she writes that Mr Elfick had received a letter from a teacher at Gylemuir Primary School asking for "someone to talk to her class of forty ten-year olds about Graysmill – I've got the job…!!! Help!". When the time came, she enjoyed the experience and was clearly at ease talking to the children, explaining about her new powerchair etc. She was also involved in "advising the Head" and entertaining the Moderator of the General Assembly of the Church of Scotland when he and entourage visited. A school coffee morning was held for a large number of invitees considering the small secondary school roll which she was actively involved in. She also tested out different sports including archery, but decided this wasn't perhaps her forte, especially when the arrow "dropped to the ground after a flight of two inches". She also had her first experience of hydrotherapy which she described as being really weird and she was a 'bit scared' but it felt pretty good on the whole when she able to more easily exercise her arms and legs. In later weeks she enjoys the experience of being completely surrounded by water. Transcribing this, reminds me of many years later while staying for a few days at Crieff Hydro, Mandy and I persuaded her to venture in to their small pool where she again experienced being gravity free, ably supported by Mandy. Somewhere there is photographic evidence which I'll probably find after this book is published.

She also describes how the university doctor, Dr Brown, came to see her at school and tried to persuade her to study through the Open University - suffice to say, this went down badly with both of them realising the error made and Suselle pointing out that she "made it clear that it just wasn't on. However, he seemed as if he will be very helpful". As I plough through the many diaries, I look forward to finding out if he was!

Graysmill School entered the NFU (National Farmers Union) annual School's Farming Project and, in her final months, a few of us worked on a large project on potatoes as our entry to the 1974 competition. Amazingly, from all the schools that entered from across Scotland, we won meaning a day at the Royal Highland Show, meeting numerous dignitaries which was something she became quite accustomed to over the years.

81

The late spring/early summer saw Suselle benefitting from the increasing freedoms and ability to spend time away from her mother exploring the area further away around her home in Dalkeith Road. Her last school day, 28th June, was very similar to that of every other Sixth Year I came to know during my own teaching career - going round bidding farewell to teachers, photos taken with staff, school friends etc, giving and receiving gifts, signing autograph books - treasured memories which so many experience. She describes herself as 'I'm a nothing' when she got home that day, with the whole of the longer summer holidays ahead of her before starting at Edinburgh University in September.

Her increasing 'sense of adventure' resulted in Leah regularly going out in the car searching for her!

In her later years, Suselle visited Taisé after finding out about it at a presentation at the then new, but now demolished St James Hotel where a BBC film "Taisé - A Place for Today" was shown in 1974.

The fuel shortages of mid 1974 meant that weekend jaunts in the car were curtailed somewhat but the summer trip south still happened starting with her first experience of Philadelphia cheese - 'like it' - en route to watch some of The Open at Lytham St Annes. The summer of 1974 saw the Higher results arrive with great trepidation as she decided whether to open them or not. In the end there was great delight as she gained an A for Geography and Bs for English and Maths meaning she had made it to Edinburgh University. Great celebrations followed along with her now annual attendance at the Church of Christ Conferences in Swanwick followed by Barnes Close. Interestingly, in one of the group sessions the topic of 'Euthanasia' was discussed - campaigning against Assisted Suicide legislation became an incredibly important part of her later life - perhaps her interest started here in the heat of a special summer.

Money was clearly tight with them having 1.5 pence to last a couple of days as the last summer holiday came to an end before starting university.

Throughout the year the arguments between mother and daughter became more acrimonious and frequent but, from her diary, appear to be almost forgotten by the next day.. most days.

In the run up to starting university, her powerchair continued to have battery problems with the odd wheel falling off to add to the mix. Even then, I think she was a bit of a jaywalker as she dashed across busy roads, often leaving people "chatting to the air!"

A few weeks before Freshers Week she received the Grant letter confirming she would be getting the full grant of £475 plus a 'new £100 allowance for disabled students'.

Ever the theatre critic, 29th August 1974 entry - "Made our way to the Lauriston Hall for Death of a Salesman by SMADS (presumably St Mary's Amateur Dramatic Society) from Newcastle. Very good. Especially liked the bloke who played Biff - Liam Neeson"!! She never mentioned that in later life.

University life started at the beginning of October with her friends Rosie and Linda learning from Leah how to lift Suselle up steps. Adjustments were made to move some classes to accessible buildings, desks and tables were allocated to ensure as easy access as possible although some lecture theatres were down three steps and up twenty-two! The full first day of term on 7th October was met with "stomach churning excitement". Her second day at Biblical Studies was her very first experience of taking notes and, she writes that she discovered later that she had misspelled some words...shock horror as this is the first time since her first diary aged seven that she has encountered spelling errors! They certainly didn't transfer to the diary.

Throughout her diaries from childhood, school and at university, she kept a record of TV programmes she watched each day which gives an insight into her extensive viewing habits - films, dramas, children's programmes and so much more.

Dr Wirz, the university doctor, was clearly an important support, probably for Leah as well as Suselle, and her fellow students and servitors shared lifting Suselle in her chair up flights of stairs to lectures, tutorials, libraries etc with her, very quickly, settling into university life and the very active Christian side of it too.

In her first year, she mentions Ian Telfer who, along with other hospital chaplains in later years, were to be an important support and providers of spiritual strength during her difficult times in hospital when she had spells of critical illness.

In November 1974, Leah started working in Teviot Refectory 10.00 a.m.-12.00 noon each day. I think this was a shock to Suselle, however, as Leah would normally come to assist Suselle with toiletting, perhaps it wasn't so surprising to others.

There is a real sense of her dedication both to her sociological and biblical studies through lectures, tutorials, Medsoc, Christian Union (CU) and more and very quickly her social life increased to what seems a whirlwind.

She makes specific mention of a Sociology lecture on inequality which makes me wonder if this was the lighting of the flame that would burn so strongly throughout her life.

I was taken right back to childhood/teenage years as she wrote of the Christmas shopping night for disabled people, (probably referred to as 'the handicapped' then), in the Woolworths store on Princes Street, on the first Monday evening in December.

1975 : Throughout the year, evening Bible reading and notes continued along with television listings!

The university technicians seemed to play a large part in keeping her powerchair going, ably arranged by Leah and the servitors. She also became Worship Secretary for Methsoc. Money was regularly in short supply as they often ran out of petrol and the car frequently broke down.

She had increasing difficulty writing long essays and asked for extensions for submissions which Leah was not happy about. In April they were 'fortunate enough' to travel 1st class on a 2nd class ticket as it was too far for Leah to carry Suselle from the guard's van where her chair was stowed otherwise they would have had to travel in the guard's van. This was a regular occurrence for wheelchair users in the past, irrespective of the season or the distance to be travelled. Towards the end of first year, her confidence is clearly growing "First Sociology tutorial this term wasn't bad. I didn't say much, but what I did say was quite brilliant!!" However, two weeks later, at the same tutorial, she describes discussing Milliband, Capitalism, Marx, pluralism as all being behind her and she felt an 'absolute idiot, but didn't open my mouth to prove it'.

As Suselle started to become slightly more independent, supported by friends and colleagues at university and elsewhere there were, naturally, strains in the mother/daughter relationship as there may be in the lives of so many.

She describes sitting in an older couples' home reading their thirty-year old "Life" magazines as "fascinating". This is partly what I'm experiencing forty years on - ploughing through her diaries. Becoming an adult brings responsibilities and she voted for the first time on 5th June this year on the Common Market. She also listened a few days later to the first ever House of Commons live radio broadcast - "now we know how the country is run", she wrote: I wonder if much has changed over the years. Another example of changed times shows when she was watching the Golf Open on television with players showing their nerves by the number of cigarettes they smoked.

1976 : Starts with Suselle full of the cold, a severe chest infection, ongoing sad scenes with Leah and not even being lifted by getting 82% in her Psychology exam. Her days at university were long, with her being there at 9.00 a.m., home for tea and frequently back to the library to study. This year, she also took part in her first radio interview on Radio Forth about the Mobility Allowance. I wonder what she would make of the current stressful situation as so many disabled people struggle to get benefits to which they are genuinely entitled.

International travel is mooted for the first time when her mum tells her she has been researching going to the USA in the summer, but Suselle writes that she doesn't think it isn't likely financially but does prepare by writing to the British Embassy in Washington regarding visiting a Congressional session while there. There are regular Friday concerts and others at the Usher Hall, going backstage of course to meet conductors, performers etc. Her home study is focused, with classical music playing in the background. There seemed to be some problems getting her placements organised mainly due to access issues - one possibility being at the Andrew Duncan Clinic doing unpaid social work but would have meant being carried up to the first floor for the whole day (no lift) or doing organised voluntary work at the Royal Edinburgh Hospital where she would have the run of the hospital. Throughout the year, her essays results improve but she also reports getting a few parking tickets, something that became a more regular occurrence in the years to come!

At her annual Swanwick Conference she realises she wanted training in Personal Lay Evangelism. Later in the summer she took delivery of a new powerchair as the previous one had become so unreliable with parts falling off, breaking down etc.

She describes an interesting 'nightmare' involving driving and then breaking down on a steep isolated road with a precipice on one side and a steep cliff on the other, which almost came true many years later while driving in Norway on one of her expeditions abroad with Mandy and Vicki.

"Our Trip to the United States of America, 4th-25th September, 1976" Journal: Saturday, 4th September 1976 saw Suselle and Leah undertaking the biggest adventure of their lives - to the USA in its bicentennial year. On waking on the day of departure, Suselle writes that she had no real feelings at all on waking this morning - "any regret about leaving my 'chariot' behind was evenly tempered with growing excitement". Auntie Agnes and Uncle Eric drove them to Glasgow Airport, where their Icelandair flight was 1½ hours late with knock on consequences. Stopping off at Keflavik, they discovered the last flight to New York had left - meaning an unexpected overnight in Iceland. Foodie Suselle describes her first Icelandic meal in their plush hotel in Reykjavik of fried halibut and shrimps with herb butter, Icelandic pancakes - flamed at our table by a very dexterous waiter! Discovering that there wouldn't be any English-speaking Church Services in Reykjavik the next morning, they went on the sightseeing bus tour instead, paid for by the airline. She describes this as a peculiar 'spiritual' decision to make hoping it was the right one but they both enjoyed the tour, getting back to the hotel at lunchtime for a brief rest before being collected and taken back to the airport for the early evening flight.

Parts of this holiday journal really deserve being quoted as Suselle's descriptive skills and sense of lifetime firsts are evident.

"I found myself inwardly urging the pilot to 'let her go' as we inched our way down the runway, and was duly satisfied with a thoroughly exhilarating feeling as we took off. I must like flying!... A couple of hours or so after taking off, the sea of clouds disappeared, and the pilot informed us that we were over Greenland. We could see lakes and rivers of ice and barren mountains - fascinating... Later, we were witnesses to a stupendous sunset, the red and golden rays stretching out along the horizon, the brilliant orb itself slowly sinking out of sight." Arriving at JFK, they were met by friends, Lora and Pat who took them to their hotel 'The Empire' -"a fairly downgrade place with black paint on woodwork, it'll serve its purpose adequately for us". Their first breakfast on US soil was in the hotel coffee shop and consisted of cheese omelette and chips, toast and coffee then the adventure began after some morning television. Look out the Big Apple here comes Suselle! Starting with a dusty walk along Columbus Avenue to 8th, drank a root beer ("wasn't impressed by the drink") before finding the World Mission Centre (WMC) where they chatted to Susan from Texas and found out that they were having a mission in Washington DC on the 18th "perhaps we'll get to it. The WMC has one basic goal: to unite all nations in Christian love... The lobby was like an oasis in the midst of a sandstorm". Later when they arrived in Washington DC and met up with their friend, Val, they were to discover during "one disturbing topic of conversation... about the 'Moonies'... we told Val of our encounter with the WMC in NY and she immediately recognized what they were. When she explained the basic aims and theology behind the 'Moonies' and the Unification Church, we were horrified; I felt so sad, because I'm sure a great number of people, like the girl we spoke to, are going to and have already, accepted this ministry of 'love' in all sincerity. Oh God, how we need discernment". The WMC was followed by more exploring that took them to the top of the Empire State Building, carried up and down the last few steps to the top by other tourists, including two friends from London and Chesterfield... "it's nice living in a small world!"; more walking to Macy's, Times Square, Broadway then back to their hotel.

Leaving later in the day to head to Boston, they discovered that NYC chequered cabs weren't the easiest way for a wheelchair user to travel to the Greyhound bus terminal. "A rather unpleasant hour ensued. On the platform, beside the Boston bus, a handful of officials materialised to inform us that it's against the rules for Greyhound staff to carry me onto the buses... (and the travel agent was supposed to have checked everything all the way through...?). Mum got increasingly frustrated and upset - as the minutes wore on, she was all for going home, and no joking. Can't say I was all that enamoured with the States for a while either."

87

There were some angels in disguise also going to Boston, who offered to carry her on and off the bus but officialdom saw to it that they didn't catch the bus as planned. "Another journeying mercy appeared in the shape of a cheery bus driver, not ours sadly; it was he who finally lifted me into a bus, mopping up unshed tears in the process. He's a Bostonian piper and has played in Scotland many times. He's with the Stewart pipers and will be in Edinburgh again next summer...I promised to look out for him!"

Hours later they arrived in Boston for three days, to be met by the Terminal Manager, Mr Karp, who lifted her off the bus then along with another 'guy' (she's picking up the Americanisms) they kindly helped them along to the cafeteria with their luggage. The walk from the bus terminal to the Avery Hotel was difficult as Leah was pushing Suselle in her wheelchair while pulling their luggage too, but at times helpful locals pushed Suselle or took the case along the route to the hotel. The next day, their pre-booked Greyhound tour of the sights of Boston was "superb", ably helped by the "marvellous guidesmanship and assistance of Herb, the driver" who carried her on and off at various points of the tour... "heading out of the City, the houses, with their open lawns and usually white-painted wooden exteriors, suggested an abundance of $ bills, but they also seemed to me to exude friendliness and simple comforts." Whilst the others explored at the various tour stop offs, Suselle stayed on board chatting to Herb who told her "of his wartime experiences in Greenock, where he couldn't understand the first native he met!" The next day, their Grayline tour to Plymouth and the Mayflower II, wasn't as enjoyable an experience but a couple of fellow passengers lifted her on and off. Back in Boston they tried out taxis with varying success, with one of the drivers being a new cabbie having "quit social work because he got tired with it", they visited Harvard University where she bought a Harvard sweatshirt. The next day they boarded a Greyhound back to NYC helped by Mr Karp again who promised to call the NYC terminal to ensure they wouldn't have the same bad experience when they had left. On arrival back in New York, Suselle describes being treated like a VIP with staff taking them both plus luggage to a taxi where the grinning driver held out his hand and 'slapped' hers. Their "two helpers shooed him away...as he replied he'd seen people in wheelchairs walk at the command of God. Interesting experience."

After checking back in to The Empire, hungry, they set off following their noses in search of a 'McDonald's' they'd seen close by! Not having these auspicious eateries in Scotland back then this was a new culinary experience and both "were surprised by the 'carry out system': the wrapped food can be eaten either outside or at the tables provided. The French fries were good!" I have a feeling that Suselle would be shocked at me including this in the story of a life well lived.

Spending time at various churches including Canaan House and Calvary Baptist in the local area was an important recharging and refreshing part of these few days in The Big Apple with new friendships made and promises of future contacts.

On 13th September, the intrepid duo set off on the Washington Express bound for more pastures new and friend, Val, who met them at the bus terminal in her little blue Volkswagen to take their case while they walked to the Midtown Motor Inn five-minutes' walk away but against the advice of their friend and one of the Greyhound staff who described the area as a 'rough one'. They had no trouble "- we have the Lord on our side!" Reading this, reminds me of when I was in Washington DC twenty years later and was given exactly the same advice when my friend and I decided to walk from our hotel to a smart restaurant beside the Potomac River. We chatted to locals as we meandered, probably as Suselle would have done all those years before.

On a whirlwind nighttime tour of the Capitol in Val's car, the White House is described as "so small", THE Monument, almost the Lincoln Memorial as they couldn't find a way round the front, the Iwo Jima Monument, the entrance to Arlington Cemetery, the University of Georgetown, Jefferson Memorial and the Tidal Basin were all excitedly seen.

14th September sees the pair up, packed and out to catch an early Greyhound for the six-hour journey to Natural Bridge, Virginia via the famous Blue Ridge Mountains which Suselle describes as only vastly wooded hills really. No more issues at the bus terminals so far, thanks to Leah making contact with each manager the day before they arrived to ensure appropriate assistance was in place to make the journey as painless as possible. Their regular service bus was a little uncomfortable and stopped at or travelled through Newington, Midlothian, Edinburg (a one street town), Glasgow and Aberdeen. Considering changes to a different bus the next day, their driver willingly promised to help make the journey more comfortable. Arriving at Natural Bridge they made their way to The Natural Bridge Motor Inn to ready for the evening outdoor performance of 'The Drama of Creation', devised by a minister for his daughter's thirteenth birthday which had taken place twice nightly every night since 1927 when President Calvin Coolidge inaugurated "The Drama of Creation," a light show that transformed the site into a nighttime destination. They felt as if they were in the south due to the heat and dialects of locals and enjoyed listening to genuine Blue Grass music entertaining delegates at a conference in their hotel. The next day their bus driver of yesterday picked them up at the hotel and, arriving at Lexington, he carried her to their next bus whose driver wasn't so communicative, taking them to Richmond where a different driver took the tourists to Williamsburg. Once there, their hotel provided a comfortable room, "sandwiches (that filling American meal) and coffee in the cool 'New Orleans' lounge - served by girls who wouldn't pass granny's test of decency! We left soon after the band struck up"!! Her birthday was celebrated taking another bus trip to Jamestown with the driver lifting her in her chair into the bus. It's not clear whether she sat in the wider aisle for the whole journey but on arrival they learned what life was like 'back in the old country' at the turn of the sixteenth/seventeenth centuries and, embarrassingly but memorably for Suselle, Leah took every opportunity to tell people that it was her daughter's twentieth birthday as they wandered through and soaked up the colonial atmosphere of Williamsburg finding it almost realistic rather than contrived. The good wishes of everyone they encountered that day made her realise that that day really was her birthday. The next day saw the start of the long way home via Greyhound to Washington DC meeting up with Val again for more night sightseeing. A quick morning tour of the White House before heading off to catch their next Greyhound, sadly her wonderful holiday journal stops at this point so I have no idea what else she did before arriving home on 25th September.

However, flowing from her journal it is clear to read that she had well and truly caught the travel bug now.

1978 : No doubt in preparation for trips abroad, Suselle attended French night classes to brush up her skills from all those years ago at school.

1979 : As a trainee social worker, she was working and learning in the area of children and families fostering and adoption with all that involves and meant visits to hospitals, prisons, young offenders institutions etc to meet with parents of children she was responsible for, meetings with Women's Aid, running family workshops, visiting children at home, in school, writing Social Background Reports for Children's Hearings, attending Children's Hearings, working with others to prepare the annual fostering campaign, exploring work possibilities and supporting those due to leave school.

The late 1970s early 1980s saw the rise of glue sniffing in Scotland, which had a major impact on the lives of many vulnerable young people. As a result, Suselle, the trainee social worker along with all other professionals working with youngsters attended various seminars to enable them to be aware of the signs to look for and ways to support families.

1980 : As a second-year trainee social worker, this year saw her moving to work in the field of elderly care based at the Royal Victoria Hospital and visiting other units and hospitals, as part of her ongoing training to becoming a qualified social worker. Despite her relative newness to the profession, she was clearly thriving and had quickly become a totally dedicated professional constantly developing her skills and experience, being involved in assessing and supporting elderly people for admission to residential houses along with counselling and following them and their families up during the transition process.

In her area team she was given responsibility for developing the post of liaison worker with a local Children's Centre, in addition to the 'normal' casework and office duties such as researching and developing the office information and resource bank.

Preparing for her annual staff evaluation, she writes movingly this year of some of the harder parts of her working life which left her with a "current loss of confidence", of finding it difficult to reconcile herself "and her clients to the compromises which all too often must be made",

91

something that she would experience herself in years to come. Being part of a team was new and something she found she had to work at and, perhaps due to physical access issues, she found very little opportunity to work with social work colleagues. Along with many other disabled people, then and now, she writes when dealing with non-social work staff, of feeling "hard put to see her social worker role when swamped by their medical model" thinking of her and of feeling threatened when her work was on view to other professions - "they're generally supportive, but sometimes their lack of knowledge is more of a hindrance", "the insensitivity of others, their non-awareness of the effect on me, leading to my current loss of confidence - immobility means I am given very few opportunities to take risks". Her weekly supervision sessions seemed to be having a more negative than positive impact on her, finding them "honest but painful". I remember in years to come, when she took on leadership roles in disabled people-led organisations and as a PA employer, her supervision sessions of others were something she took a great deal of time preparing for, and she was clearly wanting her supervision of others to be more beneficial to them than some of hers had been.

Throughout all of these complex issues, she drew on her strong Christian faith and unwound attending concerts, going to Millport, tennis championships at Wimbledon, the annual faith conference at Swanwick, the theatre and cinema. Specially highlighted days in her 1980 diary were 26th August - "*END OF PLACEMENT AND TRAINEESHIP*" and 8th September "Start of course!", I assume this is her postgrad diploma.

The end of the year notes look like something is in the planning for 1981-"phone OSC British High Commission"!

1981 : Regularly attending the Disability Income Group and Social Work Christian Fellowship. 24th July - end of placement and course. 1st December - **start work**

1982-1988 : The intervening years of diaries to 1989 are either missing or have little in them.

1989 : Suselle is at the forefront of establishing the Disability Movement in Scotland with LCDP holding its inaugural meeting in April. She also writes of attending the Edinburgh Book Festival in August.

1990, 1990, 1991 : Diaries are more challenging. Despite writing less, she writes two years on the same page. At the start of the year a Mrs Gordon advises her to write a book. Oh Suselle, if only you had, my life would have been easier but I would have missed out on the privilege of reliving our shared, varied and extraordinary life experiences over our fifty-year friendship.

Suselle is heavily involved in the disability movement and disability rights with LCDP planning the official opening by Alasdair Darling of their first base in Johnston Terrace.

Leah receives an invite to a reception with the Israeli ambassador.

Throughout her life, Taizé chants and prayer continued to invigorate through a few brief words in her private diaries.

Her holiday this year is to Ireland with Leah and Rainbow, their beloved dog and includes reading about her friend, Mike Scott (of The Waterboys) in the RTÉ Guide. During the holiday she maintains the diary of TV programmes and films seen.

Over the years, Suselle writes fondly of the importance of her 'true friendship' with Ruth, their walks, their talks, the support and difference this deep friendship means to both of them at good and difficult times.

1991 : Suselle writes of applying to the Independent Living Fund for funding to employ her own staff to take over the personal care role that her mother has done.

LCDP now have groups in each of the four local Edinburgh and Lothian areas which she is also heavily involved in and also writes that Marnie Roadburg is appointed Co-ordinator of the newly established Lothian Centre for Independent Living, which is still in existence today, doing incredible work in the field. Another offshoot of LCDP, DATE (I think this was Disability Awareness Training Edinburgh) reconstituted as Independent Disability Equality and Awareness Lothian (IDEAL) Training. The new high-quality training was established and driven by an active core group including the late Disability Rights activist and good friend, Neil Robinson. She describes the IDEAL meetings as always being relaxed and positive.

Late March sees her briefly noting another chest infection which needs daily physio home visits.

Suselle still manages to keep actively involved in Church matters etc despite all her other commitments. She writes that she attended both days of Mission 91 (Billy Graham) at Murrayfield Stadium where she and I met again for the first time in a few years, renewing a special friendship that was to last until her death.

Working in Fostering and Adoption, she writes movingly of the struggles of finding suitable families for sibling groups to keep them together, the ongoing lack of resources issues for children and being back to 'nil' resources, an all too familiar situation in the current day too as I write this, negatively impacting social work staff, families and others supporting vulnerable children and young people.

She writes of watching the "One in Four" series on television about the Nazi view of disability - that disabled people were "useless eaters". These disturbing facts would have been written out of Disability History without the growing Disability Movement which continues to campaign for the basic rights that Suselle held so dear. The following programme in the series was on current theories of euthanasia but disappointingly she hasn't written about this.

For the first time, she spends two-week respite time at Mayfield House which she benefited from, and, encouraged by her work colleagues, is actively considering a holiday in Colorado.

Something that isn't so straightforward to do now due to security measures, were her regular visits to the airport for tea and, of course, to watch the planes. Over the summer she writes of seeing Pat Duncan on television on "Scottish Women" on transport.

17th September sees the tragic death in a car crash of two friends, Mark and Lottie Cheverton who founded the Leith School of Art which was to be a beneficiary of Suselle's 'estate'. This tragedy struck Suselle, many of her friends and the Ps & Gs community hard and on the following Sunday her diary entry is "Excellent Service, centred on Mark and Lottie - Roger, virtually in tears, preached all the more powerfully on the Lazarus story. This may be a real turning point for the Church and for individuals (found myself thinking about starting that book...)" I found more information on Mark and Lottie here: http://www.heraldscotland.com/arts_ents/13157544.Memories_mix_melancholy_with_pride/

September sees the determined drive to employ PAs for the first time and following a meeting a few days later she writes of what, with hindsight, I think may have become a pivotal life changing meeting with an Archie Ramsay "to discuss how he's gone about employing carers. Useful and relaxed." During the month, with support and advice from Pat Black she 'words an ad, prepares an application from, job description etc. Pat always leaves me feeling fairly positive...'. Once the advert, job description etc are finalised, with things looking finally close to getting under way, she writes of feeling 'quite excited as well as terrified'... This preparation came at the right time as Leah had a fall which caused a lot of back pain, resulting in days off work for Suselle. Leah was struggling with assisting her to get up so Suselle got some overnight 'help' from an agency in the city to make both their lives more manageable.

November sees the official launch of LCiL. Interestingly, on the day in November when she receives the very first application form re her PA job (not from Mandy yet), she writes of watching 'the old film "Mandy"'!! Her first ever PA, Linda Robertson, is appointed in December to start early in the new year.

1992 : First overseas trip since employing PAs to Holland in April with Leah and PA Linda for the European Symposium on 'the Church and Disability' in Holland where she met and was inspired by Joni Earekson Tada.

1997 : Diaries from this year onwards are purely standard work and general appointment diaries.

2002 : Period of time in hospital to 18th February with severe chest infection. Learning to use Voicetext.

2003 : Direct payments meetings.

2007 : Homegroup is an important part of Suselle's life. Work, now a social worker working in direct payments, although I'm not entirely sure when the shift happened, involved covering the advice line, carrying out home visits, supporting and encouraging others to remain independent and taking part in PA employer interviews.

Increasingly hospital visits and health issues become more of a norm with diabetic clinics, sleep clinics, eye hospital and other appointments. With the onset of dementia, Leah requires specialized care and Suselle is involved in taking Leah to visit care homes. She moved into Castlegreen Care Home in December 2007, where she was to be well-cared for and remain for the rest of her life which was a great relief for Suselle, who remained involved in ensuring that high quality care was important by attending various meetings in Castlegreen, bringing her life and professional expertise to the table.

This is the last paper diary I had access to but in the forty-three years of diaries I have had the privilege of reading, they give a vivid sense of her life as she grew from a young seven-year old enrolling in the Brownies, to the dedicated, humane, devout Christian and dearest friend, colleague and more than that to hundreds, if not thousands. Her legacy will continue to make a real difference to the lives of many at home and overseas for many years to come. Hers truly was 'A Life Well-Lived'.

THE LETTER
(copied into one of the diaries)

Spare time to write, and do not send a careless scribble to your friend.
Don't fill the pages with your blues - first, think of all the cheerful news!
Don't let yourself intrude too much, and keep a sunny-tempered touch;
No letter to a friend should be filled with complaints and misery.
Do not forget to dip your pen in laughter's sunshine, now and then;
Let loving kindness be your guide, as if your friend was at your side.

Anne Hope

Ditties
from school jotters

Day

Eyes flutter open; now I must rush;
Switch on Tony Blackburn; hurriedly dress;
Eat some breakfast; there is no hush;
What time is there? none, even less.

Cram books into schoolbag; dash to the door;
Run back for blazer; now I am out.
Nearly at school; a few strides more
In the playground, one of the girls shouts.

The school bell rings; children file in;
The clatter of footsteps is on the stairs;
And in the classroom; now there's no din,
Because the teachers are there in their lairs.

School is over, homework done.
We go out now; with our friends
Into the fresh air, enjoying fun.
Of another day, it is almost the end.

Limerick

There was a small feline named Sooty
Who stole all the bad pirate's booty,
She was put in a jail,
Then a boy pulled her tail,
And she kicked him with her neat
little footy.

Tea

Tea
Everyone drinks it
Well, not everyone.
Most
What is tea?
Some leaves?
A drink?
Both?
Yes
Reversed, it is eat
No, not reversed
Mixed
Anyway, you don't eat tea.
It is drunk
Tea

Records I'd Like

Back Home : England World Cup Squad
Everything is Beautiful : Ray Stevens
The Spirit in the Sky : Norman Greenbaum
Water Town : Frank Sinatra
Glen Campbell Live
Try a little Kindness : Glen Campbell
Bridge over troubled Water : Simon and Garfunkel

Award-winning Letter of the Week
Radio Times November 2004
A Commentary on Mr Donald Trump and Mammon

LETTER OF THE WEEK

Greed isn't good

Having followed the first US series of *The Apprentice* (BBC2) with growing dismay, I wondered whether other viewers shared my love/hate response to this foray into unrestrained capitalism. On one level, we were asked to follow Donald Trump's insistence that he was looking for the clean and respectable qualities of leadership and initiative. At the same time, we were asked to suspend all

MICHAEL SHEEHY

values except the profit motive – although this was not once acknowledged, of course. Never a mention of the good of the community or taking care of the environment. Always a focus on the obscene opulence of Trump's corporate developments (which only the wealthiest of Americans can afford to enter, I suspect).

I seethed at the injustice of it all, and I truly worried at the superficial values these incredibly able young people were being asked to uphold, and in such an irresistible ambience of competitiveness. Surprise, surprise – the "winner" was a white, upper-class man – no change to the status quo there.

We can only hope the British version does not follow suit.

Suselle Boffey, Edinburgh

PURE DIGITAL

Ms Boffey wins a digital radio – Pure's Bug, designed with Wayne Hemingway, lets you pause, rewind and record live radio. It's available to buy for only £149.99 plus £3.49 p&p. Call **0870 062 6263,** *quoting ref LP12. Check digital radio availability in your area at www.ukdigitalradio.com/coverage or call 0870 010 0123.*

7
Legacy of a life well-lived

And so *Suselle's Story* is in print. School jotters and other memorabilia which Leah and Suselle stored for sixty years have been deposited with The Living Memory Association (THELMA), which makes up life-story "school bags" as teaching-tools available on loan to schools and organisations. Within the first few months on line, there had been around five-thousand viewings.

In accordance with the instructions to her trustees, the proceeds of Suselle's estate were distributed to local and international charities, with a condition that the funds would be allocated to improving access facilities for people with mobility issues. One of the charities, World Vision, used the bequest for a project in Bangladesh which helps very poor and marginalised single mothers, widows and disabled children who are still being hidden away because of being deemed to have brought shame on the family.

Suselle was not hidden from the world – Leah's resources and resourcefulness were dedicated to introducing Suselle to a world of adventure and purpose which Suselle embraced and lived to the full to become, as Jane Campbell so aptly describes in the Foreword ...*the woman who travelled great distances, breaking-down or circumventing enormous barriers along the way.*